MEET YOUR MATCH

If you want to know how ...

365 Steps to Self-Confidence

A programme for personal transformation in just a few minutes a day

Tracking Down Your Ancestors

Discover the story behind your ancestors and bring your family history to life

Planning Your Wedding

A step-by-step guide that will take you right through to the big day

Making a Wedding Speech

How to face the big occasion with confidence and carry it off with style

Times of My Life

The definitive guide for writing your life story

howtobooks

Please send for a free copy of the latest catalogue to:
How To Books
3 Newtec Place, Magdalen Road,
Oxford OX4 1RE, United Kingdom
email: info@howtobooks.co.uk
www.howtobooks.co.uk

Meet Your Match

How to find and keep the man or woman who's right for you

Jennie Hawthorne

Published by How To Books Ltd,
3 Newtec Place, Magdalen Road,
Oxford OX4 1RE, United Kingdom.
Tel: (01865) 793806. Fax: (01865) 248780
Email: info@howtobooks.co.uk
www.howtobooks.co.uk

First edition 2005
Reprinted 2005

British Library Cataloguing in Publication Data.
A catalogue record for this book is available from the British Library

Produced for How To Books by Deer Park Productions, Tavistock
Typeset by Pantek Arts Ltd, Maidstone, Kent
Printed and bound in Great Britain by Bell & Bain Ltd, Glasgow

NOTE: The material contained in this book is set out in good faith for general guidance and no liability can be accepted for loss or expense incurred as a result of relying in particular circumstances on statements made in this book. The laws and regulations are complex and liable to change, and readers should check the current positions with the relevant authorities before making personal arrangements.

Contents

Preface – or How This Book Got Its Title

My husband Frank Hawthorne and his friend Mike Myers, senior maths lecturers, enjoyed a game of chess. They often played together in the college staff room during their lunchtime break.

On one occasion the two men, both reasonably good players, accepted a challenge by their teacher colleagues to enter a competition taking place in nearby Croydon.

The two men set off for the large exhibition hall where the chess matches were to be held. Never having visited the place before, they wandered round the first floor searching for the venue. A woman came out of the lift, eyed them up and suddenly ran towards them.

'Are you going to the Meet and Match?' she asked, a tremor of hope in her voice.

Quick as a flash Mike replied, 'No, sorry, we're going to the Meet and Mate.' Whether Frank and Mike won the tournament, I do not know, but the above story partly explains this book's origin and title. Its aim is to help you meet, marry and stay with the right man or woman for you.

Jennie Hawthorne

Introduction

Are you looking for friends, a partner you might grow to love? Already met somebody you want to see more of, but who doesn't feel the same way about you? Perhaps you prefer the company of your own sex? Or it may be that your marriage has already floundered in a sea of hope and appears to be heading for the rocks, your partner incapable of understanding you. Then this book is for you.

To win someone's heart, you don't have to be the most popular person on the campus, the most beautiful woman/handsome man around. Los Angeles is reputed to do more nip and tuck operations than anywhere else in the world and you can take your pick (no pun intended) of: surgery to alter the shape of your chin, lift up your forehead, get rid of the bags under your eyes, or the collagen on your thighs; procedures to fatten or thin your lips; a botox session for your face and augmentation of your breasts. Judging by the number of Dolly Parton look-alikes in LA this appears to be the most popular method of winning your way to a man's heart.

Why go in for these expensive nose and other jobs that some fashion writers so subtly recommend you wonder if they run plastic surgery clinics as a sideline? Unless there is a really radical problem or disability, ignore these appeals to your ego. If you feel good and attractive in your own eyes, other people will think the same – no need to visit surgeons to disguise the fact that you've been circumcised (don't ask me how or why it's done), pin your ears down, change your nose, puff out your lips, enlarge/reduce your breasts, or perform other miracles … for a price.

No need either to spend a fortune on a first date. According to research commissioned by Virgin in 10 different UK regions, single men spend an average of £186.10 on this momentous occasion. Often it's all for a big zero. A reader of the national statistics magazine *Horizons* asked in 2003 if this expenditure was really necessary. He writes: 'I've had to ensure that my wife doesn't see this figure as we just went for a drink on our first date, although a single female colleague of mine has photocopied it and placed it around our building to ensure prospective suitors know the standards expected.'

No similar spending statistics are yet available for women. Yet why should anybody go on a frenzied shopaholic spree to win somebody's heart by buying the most expensive outfits in London, New York or Paris? There are far more satisfying methods of winning minds and sometimes hearts to go with them. Author Sophie Kinsella paints a different picture in her hilarious shopaholic books, but then the heroine can be forgiven, as she is already halfway to the altar.

Maureen Rees, the Cardiff cleaner who came to fame as a learner driver with her husband Dave in the British TV series, *Driving School,* confessed she never went out much with anyone before Dave because she thought she looked like the back of a bus. But when Dave, four years her junior, met her on a blind date he was immediately attracted by her lovely smile. Six months later they were married.

Other stories in this book are equally inspiring. They show that it doesn't matter whether you are fit or not, plain or beautiful, have a string of failed relationships behind you, or even one looming up in front, you can still find AND KEEP Mr. or Ms. Right without losing your self respect ... or your savings. The following pages may not set you on a walk to the altar with Walter ... or Laura, but they open up other options, equally satisfying and life enhancing.

They give examples, for different ages, of ways to meet people. Case histories show how such meetings were converted into longer term relationships. Danger signs and cautionary tales help prevent readers of both sexes being conned by smooth talkers who are not always what they seem, and who can rob gullible listeners of their savings, confidence and self esteem. So read on ...

Chapter 1 outlines the present state of matrimony, family life ... and divorce.

Chapter 2 investigates how these trends have come about and how both men and women are losing out through the search for an equality that defies biology.

Chapter 3 looks at 'singles' and suggests they think carefully before giving up their present lifestyle for something different. That may not be the answer. You may be old (when does that apply?), wondering whether a bit of company and affection might be preferable to living alone waiting for the phone to ring. You may be young and getting back to your lonely bedsit after a hard day's work and wondering what advantages there are in being on your own. On the other hand, with several flatmates sharing the kitchen sink and practically everything else, the idea of just one partner seems like paradise.

You may have passed your vernal youth, had one or more relationships that have all gone sour, or – it happens – none at all. Now you appear to have everything: interesting career, plenty of friends (most of them married), plenty of cash and a home of your own, but something is missing. Could it be a new outlook, man, woman ... or even (hush, hush) a pet?

The trouble is that as you get older, you become more 'choosy' than you were in your twenties and there are less people around who come up to your expectations. Those that do have already been snatched up. Madeleine Albright, the first female US Secretary of State, confesses that she would have given up any thought of a career if it could have persuaded her husband of 23 years to stay with her. But when asked, in an interview with Catherine O'Brien, if she would like to meet somebody fabulous and sexy, she replied, 'Absolutely. But I have to tell you they are not exactly hanging around out there.'

Exactly. But don't let any diminution in the supply of the fabulous and sexy cause you to lower your sights and rush in where virgins fear to tread. You might find yourself one of a miserable twosome and then ... a miserable onesome. There are happier and more worthwhile options than that. When thinking of tying the nuptial knot, think again. As Benjamin Franklin wrote in *Poor Richard's Almanack*, 'Keep your eyes wide open before marriage, half shut afterwards.'

And King Vidor said of marriage it was 'not a word but a sentence'. That goes for a partnership too. As Elizabeth Taylor, Mickey Rooney, Joan Collins and others in the entertainment world have shown, a second or even a third, fourth, fifth or sixth shot does not always prove better than the first. They are not the only ones to have discovered this sobering truth. You don't want to, and unless you are so rich you don't actually know what you're worth, you can't afford to join the hundreds of thousands who plunge into matrimony or other relationship one year and try, often acrimoniously, to get out the next. Nor do you want a series of unsatisfying pairings that end up in punch-ups or tears and leave you emotionally or even physically scarred.

If after reading **Chapter 3** you still prefer to try your luck at finding a suitable partner, **Chapter 4** asks you to analyse yourself so that you can more easily make up your mind about whether you want a partner at all, and if so the ideal you're looking for and what you can give to him/her. Men's and women's needs are different. Physical attraction is the usual spark that lights up the flame of romance, passion or lust. It can set a pair on the road to heaven or to hell, or fizzle out like a damp squib. Researchers, who may know little more than you or me, tell us that we make decisions about the attractiveness of people we meet in the space of milliseconds. They do not add the relevant but ill phrased proverb that 'one man's meat is another man's poison'.

Men tend to put sex at the top of their list of what they want from a woman, certainly in the short term. They also seek somebody who is affectionate, good company, preferably good looking – at least in their view – and might even turn out to be (no harm in hoping), a good homemaker/carer/cook. These needs vary with age and situation. A widower, for example, might want somebody who, above all, will care for his children, though a sympathetic ear and other qualities will not go amiss.

Young men first notice good looks or good grooming or particular physical attributes that appeal to them. So do young women, but many of them find power, money or status equally acceptable. Most older men and women, though still vulnerable to good looks, find other assets sometimes more desirable, especially a small fortune in the bank.

For a longer relationship, there are other needs that do not depend only on gender, but on the age, character and situation of the people involved. Companionship, affection or mutual interests (such as music, chess, athletics, football, bridge, polo, travel) often prove a magnet. The desire for children sometimes overrides other considerations. A person who, in theory at least, might be able fulfil this desire, gets a high rating, lowered by previous obligations. These obligations might include an ex-partner, alimony, maintenance and debts of various kinds. Children of a previous relationship can throw a spanner in the works or oil them. Will you make a good step-parent? Take care. Children are very vulnerable, even if you are not.

An interesting St. Valentine's day survey by a leading insurance company suggested, surprisingly perhaps, that 'British men and women are more likely to look twice at a potential partner if they have a pension.'

Other nations may be more romantic ... or less truthful. This study of attitudes to love and money further showed that over 43% of men admitted they were attracted to women with long-term financial security such as a pension of their own, while nearly 48% of the women questioned said men with long-term financial security have an 'attractive presence about them' (the scent of money?).

Nearly 70% of women declared the prospect of financial security was an important part of romance, while only 49% of men looking for the ideal partner rated this factor as important. A further light on the unromantic attitude of women was shed by the fact that 64% said they would like their ideal partner to be able to keep them in the manner to which they want to become accustomed (!) while only 49% of the men had this attitude. True love apparently lasts only if the money does not run out. Believe it or not as you like (bearing in mind who commissioned the survey).

Research for a giant electrical appliance company gave a little more romantic and other information specifically about Londoners: 84% of them rated good health as their top priority for a good quality life, with only 47% opting for being loved; 37% wanted a satisfying job; 28% low stress levels and 22% spiritual well-being. Having plenty of money was rated as a top need for a good quality life by only 15% of Londoners, 5% below the national average. (Perhaps those questioned had enough already.)

If after reading all these facts and figures, you still want to find a soulmate, **Chapter 5** supplies a huge array of places where you can meet people as well as details of organisations (including the Internet) which help you to do this and their cost. (Some are free.) It also gives examples of people who have trodden this route for better or worse.

Before trying any of these paths to an earthly paradise, however, go on to **Chapter 6**. This should prevent you from arriving, before your time, at a heavenly paradise instead. It stresses the need for safety when arranging or keeping a date, and suggests precautions to prevent you from taking a wrong turning or making a wrong choice. Some cautionary tales are included.

Chapter 7 shows ways of making a good first impression, how to improve your communication skills, how to hold and keep a listener's attention, and develop and improve relationships.

Chapter 8 assumes you have found your match. It asks some searching questions about various kinds of relationships. Is marriage the answer? If so, what is its purpose? Is it preferable to 'living together'? What about people of the same sex? And what of the financial, legal and other aspects affecting different types of partnerships? Seriously consider the options.

Chapter 9 outlines danger signs that occur in any relationship, the capital sins which lead to hell, while **Chapter 10** gives the contrary virtues which can lead to a temporary heaven and illustrates them with well-tried examples. **Chapter 11** deals with problem-solving and gives answers from those who have dealt with such problems.

CONCLUSION

With a bit of luck thrown in for good measure, it is always possible, if you know yourself and what you want, to meet somebody whose company you enjoy so much that you fancy living with them for at least part of a lifetime.

Knowing what you want is the vital point. Looking for a soulmate, a partner, a kindred spirit without knowing yourself is likely to bring you more misery than joy.

Whatever your age, ability and appearance, there are all manner of choices open to you. Knowing what you want does not mean grabbing anything in sight. Such moves are more likely to lead you up the garden path than down the aisle. Flitting from flower to flower looks like a wonderfully sybaritic existence, but winter comes; there is no honey left and no hive either.

The only new beginning that comes from putting your own happiness before everything else, even when an ideal partner drops into your lap (in a manner of speaking), usually ends up as a nightmare, not a dream. Take time to consider this Trojan horse, this gift of the gods, this magical Mr. or Ms. Right who could so easily turn out to be plain Mr. or Ms. Wrong.

So there you have it – different approaches for different people; the ways to:

■ win any mating/dating game
■ create a long-lasting and happy relationship that suits YOU

OR

■ enjoy what you've got, including your independence.

Part One

FINDERS

Partnerless People:
the Current Scene

Today's marriage proposals – when made at all – come in many forms. Sometimes the mere twitch of an eyebrow is enough. For others, the route to the altar is harder. Proposals may arrive through text messages, others perhaps by TV's dateline service, which attracts at any one time some 30,000 people looking for partners. And there are numerous similar agencies, many mentioned in this book. Newspapers and magazines, however, still remain one of the easiest and most popular routes to meeting others.

'WOULD LIKE TO MEET'

Of the advertisements in these outlets, a fairly small space is taken up by Women Seeking Men, much less for Women To Women ('straight' or 'single' for 'socialising and eating out'). A bigger section comes under the heading, Men To Men. With the exception of the *Financial Times*, where readers may be more concerned with making money than dates (though both together will not come amiss), the largest column of all is usually for Men Seeking Women.

As one example, under a caption 'Ladies And Gentlemen', one upmarket paper highlights a *cri de coeur*. Beginning attractively enough 'chap 40, single, in back of beyond', the gentleman goes on to describe the object of his search – 'city based lady for cosy, cultural Christmas conversations and Tuscan hols'. But the heading 'Good cook and ironer?' leaves much unanswered. Is it the city based lady or the chap 40, single, who will do the ironing and lace the pudding with cultural Christmas conversations in the Tuscan hols? The answer may mean the beginning or end of a romance.

These few lines, like all the other adverts or a good CV, usually conceal more than they reveal and are quite unlike those once very popular in Germany. They began 'innocent divorcée' (*schuldlos geschieden*), always *schlank*. After a brief description of the required Adonis the ending comes 'with a view to marriage'. This phrase has completely disappeared from the current scene, and not only in Germany. Of almost 100 adverts under Men Seeking Women, taken at random from a large circulation London-based newspaper, there is only one reference to marriage. It comes from an Indian businessman of 27 who wishes 'to meet genuine lady for a lasting relationship, possibly marriage'. Divorce itself has become too common to be mentioned.

The 'alluring, attractive, charming, caring, affectionate' females are all seeking not marriage, but 'friendship/relationship'. This is occasionally extended to an 'honest, loving relationship'. Occasionally the word romance is mentioned and one person in a hundred may be 'genuinely looking for commitment'. The 'attractive, adventurous, assertive, affectionate, charismatic, charming, extrovert, good looking, gorgeous' men who advertise (no blushing violets here) want women for fun, friendship and laughs, romance (occasionally) and (rarely) timeless moments or (even more rarely) a life companion. Some men hedge their bets with explanatory adjectives: no strings; lasting; long term (followed by a question mark); steady; sincere, or even … solvent. When a single mother or student is mentioned, so is a 'supportive relationship', though who is supporting whom is not quite clear.

Translation guide

A dictionary of words and phrases can be useful in translating some of the messages. TLC for tender loving care is now *passé*. WLTM for 'would like to meet' is the 'in' word for an assignation. It should really add TBA, to be arranged. That escape has not yet been adopted. 'No hang ups' does not refer to the laundry. N/S is for non smoking, presumably tobacco. Somebody in a January advertisement still wants to 'pull a Christmas cracker'. The pulling is unlikely to be for the motto inside the wrapping. SOH (sense of humour) is naturally much in demand. Just as naturally but far more rarely is LTR (long term relationship).

Honesty might win over a hesitant suitor for the 40-year-old woman who 'likes being spoilt' and seeks a film star hero (tall, dark, handsome) for romance. For good measure she adds that he must be wealthy, too.

No harm in asking. Phrases like 'for genuine friendship' or 'an honest loving relationship' can cover up stranger needs. In other countries there are no such inhibitions. In California, for example, a weekly paper might publish adverts barely intelligible to the more restrained English reader:

> 'A sensuous tantrica couple want a polyfidel taoist for mind boggling erotic fun.'
> 'A wife seeks a boyfriend for her husband.'

And in the same publication there are enough hot, hot bodies on offer to curl the pages, let alone the toes of anybody brave or reckless enough to reply.

FINDERS, NOT KEEPERS

Most 'soul mate' advertisements are like the tip of iceberg. The ocean ahead may bring you shoreward soon or hide horrible hazards. Go with the floe and you will discover how sought-after are happy 'relationships', how hard it is to find them. Yet, unless you're a monk or nun in an enclosed order, meeting new people in a crowded urban world seems very easy ... sometimes too easy. So it is, especially for the very rich or the very young. Their problem is usually not so much in finding acquaintances, friends or partners; it is in avoiding or leaving them without too much hassle or grief.

Film stars can afford to move around from partner to partner, even if huge alimony settlements might be the result. Harrison Ford reputedly forked out $15m after an 18-year marriage. Michael Douglas also had to dig deep into his coffers for the divorce that legally allowed him to marry Catherine Zeta Jones. (And the first/second wives' club, no longer in their pristine youth, might well ask, why not?)

Other 'celebs' act like newly enriched tribal chiefs who do not know how to spend their money except to have more of the same. Their power is such that they get it. In Western society, men or women who have had several 'affairs' or marriages are rarely viewed as 'shifty' characters, except perhaps in the political arena. *Au contraire*, they are usually written about as if such partnerships proved only their virility or beauty, not their inconstancy. Like anglers seeking a good catch, they go trawling for a 'trophy' wife or husband. The trophy rusts and must be replaced … and so it goes on, often leaving behind sadness in their wake and sometimes a legacy of bitterness for the next generation.

If you grow tired of somebody, the message is to move on. Never mind if the person you move away from was at one time OK. They aren't any longer, so you don't stay. Never mind what promises you made. Loyalty or duty are not buzz words.

BIOLOGY VERSUS EQUALITY

The modern climate of change ignores the iron law of biology, older and far less flexible than that of sexual equality. Biology involves the sex drive, part of nature's plan for procreation. In men, that urgency is stronger than it is in women. If it didn't exist, neither would we. A plus for women, did they but know it (and some do), is that biology gives them the role of hunters or choosers when they are young-ish. They can say no as often as they like, and to as many applicants for their 'favours' as they wish. There will always be other men around hoping to catch (what used to be) the elusive, desirable female. Sadly, such are the vagaries of love, the elusive, desirable female often does not want to be caught by these 'other' men. The minus side is that in spite of all the wonderful medical advances that can assist with conception, nature cruelly, or perhaps kindly, imposes a time limit on women's fertility. And, with rare exceptions, it shows.

Anybody who does not believe this simple truth has only to ask them-selves how many older romantic heroines they see on TV, in films, plays and advertisements, compared with romantic young women or roman-tic old men? Only rare exceptions like the evergreen Calendar Girls attract as much sexual interest as younger women. Admiration and love yes, but how many calendar girls are there around anyway?

Women are unlikely at the age of 60 or 70 (unless they have oodles of money and a few new body parts) to woo and win toy boys some 30 years their junior – although it can be done. To a few, the joy of such a union is worth the effort of getting it. The pain of parting usually comes far too soon. If you must and can, have your dream, but know the score so that when it ends, as it surely will, you can sing with Piaff, *'Je ne regrette rien.'*

At the other end of the time scale, men are the winners, the choosers. Until they are 80 or more they can still procreate, and any loss of good looks or sexual attraction is usually compensated for by a bit of power, status or cash. Most men have acquired one or other or even all of these attributes over a working life of a couple of decades. As for a title or decoration, that will do wonders, especially for second time around 'monsters' so many divorcees claim to have married.

Allowing for the fact that women tend to live longer than men, marriage also appears to be of greater benefit to men than women in their old age. In the UK, 52.5% of women aged 75 to 84 live alone, while only 25.7% of men of this age range do so (National Statistics 2003). Men under 65 years head the list for the fastest increase in single households – we are becoming a nation of singles and the prediction is that by the year 2020, there will be 23% more households and one in three people living alone. Divorce and separation largely account for this trend, with people in their middle years being the most affected.

Though 300,000 hopefuls tie the knot in the UK each year, four in ten untie it, making our divorce rate the highest in Europe. The break-up rate for couples living together, not perhaps surprisingly, is even higher. In spite of the stark fact that over 30% of all children will, before they reach the age of 16, experience the parting of their natural parents, most Londoners still choose the marriage route to happiness, even if in the back of their minds, one (or both) of the partners keeps a 'cop out' clause, not a happy-ever-after one.

Marriage no longer gives the assurance (barring death) to either spouse of lasting love, companionship and care. And if men vanish when a baby appears or is likely to appear on the scene, where will they be when their *inamorata* becomes older or disabled? Certainly not by their side or pushing a wheelchair for them. Perhaps this is why there has been such a big swing away from the commitment of marriage altogether.

In the US the trend towards the end of marriage as an institution is moving faster. Marriage is almost never seen as a sacred ceremony, except in old fashioned Catholic or Jewish communities, or in films, where it lingers on because of its scenic not religious value.

Nor is marriage viewed as a civil ceremony promising a lifelong commitment, though the trimmings of reception, guests, wedding dress, bridesmaids and all the rest may remain and are often more extravagant, even bizarre. If the promises 'for richer, for poorer' are ever spoken by the spouses, the intention appears to be only for richer. And 'till divorce do us part' should in truth take the place of 'till death do us part'. In fact the only part of the marriage service which seems to mean what it says today, is 'with this body I do thee worship' – which is probably believed by the well intentioned young, at least until a better sculpted body appears on the horizon. The rich old men who marry bimbos may also mean what they say when they make such a promise. Though they are unlikely to break it, they may never be able to keep it either.

Instead of marriage being an institution which helps towards mutual affection and the raising and rearing of children, it is seen as merely one path among many in the search for personal happiness. This disappearance of marriage in favour of other lifestyles means, according to a profound remark by Maggie Gallagher of the US *Women's Quarterly*, that we are undermining 'the only institution ever shown to be capable of raising children or civilising the erotic drives of men'.

No silver threads among the golden

When people are more averse to tying the knot, it comes as no surprise that the number of golden weddings is also falling. Of an average 300,000 couples marrying each year, less than 10% are expected to reach their 50th anniversary and this in spite of the increasing longevity of both men and women. In 1947, 400,000 couples got married in the UK. Fifty years later, 28% of them (some 112,000) celebrated their golden wedding and only 10% had divorced. By contrast, 10% of those who married in the 1990s divorced in the first five years and nearly 25% within 10 years.

If this trend continues, as seems likely, what does it mean for the future? Age Concern gave a partial answer. In a survey of the ten million people born in the sixties, many were likely to do well financially in their old age because of the economic boom of the 1980s and 90s. Those without savings or personal pensions, however, faced a bleak future. The collapse of marriage, higher incidence of divorce, dispersed families and childlessness meant today's thirty-somethings could be left facing misery in their old age. If they become too ill or infirm to look after themselves, the only option appears to be expensive nursing homes.

The care for older people that often used to be provided by family members is likely to become a still rarer commodity in the future. More than one in five people remain childless and the number of children born per woman is now below replacement level, the lowest since records began in 1924. A declining proportion of taxpayers could lead to a tightening of eligibility for state care, not only for the elderly.

Statistics which highlight these findings include the following:

■ Around 18% of women and 15% of men born in 1961 saw the break-up of their marriage or relationship before they were 30.
■ Men can expect to live 21 years after retirement; women manage 25 years.
■ 12% of women and 18% of men born in the sixties will not have married nor be living with a partner by the age of 50.
■ 10% of women and 14% of men born in 1961 will still be single at 60. Figures for 30 years previously show percentages of six and eight respectively.

Perhaps new policies are needed to stem marriage breakdowns, high levels of short-term cohabitation and greater childlessness.

2

Changing Trends

When Jane Austen wrote her novel *Pride and Prejudice* in 1813, the oft-quoted opening (*It is a truth universally acknowledged, that a single man in possession of a good fortune must be in want of a wife*) showed very clearly the position of middle class women at that time.

Their future depended on men: husbands if they married, fathers or other male relatives if they did not. When they lived on an entailed estate, it passed to a male relative, however distant, when the father died. Daughters then had to leave their home and move elsewhere.

Jane Austen was lucky, for her brother who inherited the family estate supported his sister financially for a time. She knew all about the difficulties of middle class unmarried women. In spite of the touch of irony, it is a recurring theme in her books.

So Mrs Bennett, however silly she appears in *Pride and Prejudice*, had reason to be concerned about the future of her five daughters. Seen in the light of the customs of nineteenth century England, marriage was for all her girls, save the independent Elizabeth, one of their few options other than being an 'old maid'. A 'good' marriage was vitally important to them. Few jobs were available other than as a governess. In that position they were neither fish nor fowl; too well-born to be accepted downstairs, too lowly to be welcomed upstairs.

Yet even a 'good' marriage was no piece of cake. Women could not keep their own money or easily leave their husbands. If they ever managed to get a divorce (a most difficult procedure, needing the help of clever lawyers), they had no automatic right to the custody of their children. This possible deprivation was often used as a threat to recalcitrant wives.

ADULTERY AND INHERITANCE

The reason for this situation is not hard to seek. Double standards of chastity for men and women were enshrined in the laws which governed marriage and property rights in England until the late nineteenth century and in other parts of Europe until the early twentieth century. Inheritance went through the male line. Unless a baby was swapped at birth, there was no doubt as to who was its mother. For many years royal births had to be witnessed to avoid such a contingency. Blood tests were not used and DNA not yet discovered so there was no indisputable proof of fatherhood.

A wife's adultery could result in the birth of offspring not fathered by the legitimate husband. Women were therefore made the target of legal constraints. These constraints did not apply to men, for if their adulterous affairs led to unmarried women giving birth, their children were more patently illegitimate. The children could not inherit, though provision might be made for them.

Working class women were not troubled by the laws of inheritance. Marriage usually offered them (as for their richer sisters) the best option. There was no welfare state provision. Jobs paid starvation wages, but that was better than nothing. Without work, the spectre of the workhouse loomed ahead. Organised charity, with few exceptions, was, in the words of J.B. O'Reilly, 'scrimped and iced in the name of a cautious, statistical Christ'. Marriage then provided a safeguard of some kind.

The possible earning power of a husband gave to his wife and children a degree of security. By contrast a mistress, unless of a rich and very generous man (traits which do not always go together), was in a very vulnerable position, and her children might be even worse off. Until the end of the nineteenth century, 30 out of every 1,000 children still did not survive their first year.

NEW OPPORTUNITIES AND FREEDOMS

The lot of all women has altered radically since Jane Austen's day and is likely to alter still more in the twenty-first century. Contraception gives them the opportunity to have sex without the fear of bearing an illegitimate child. The concept of illegitimacy itself has gone out of the window and in Britain, abortion can be had almost on demand. Mothers need no longer fear starvation, social stigma or the workhouse for themselves or their 'bastard' children. They can have sex without marriage and even children without sex and do not have to look to the father, known or unknown, for financial support. The state will do that job if either is unemployed.

Social welfare, assisted housing or tax concessions may be miserly compared with the finances of better off parents, but such benefits ensure, at least, that no child with or without two parents need die from starvation in the Western world today.

Women do not have to be governesses or nannies, but if they choose these jobs, they are likely to earn a good salary and be respected by the wealthy families who can afford them. Neither do they have to resign jobs on marriage, as they did for example in the UK civil service and teaching, until World War Two. Some part, at least, of the world is now their oyster. Under-represented in politics, banking, the international scene, top posts in industry, academia and the civil service, women nevertheless have new career opportunities opening up to them in a way never possible even only a couple of decades ago. In theory at least it seems a woman can have everything if she has the 'right' personality – with a modicum of good looks. If both are not quite perfect, high qualifications might suffice. This means a longer period of study to get those qualifications. To rise higher in their chosen career, women post-pone marriage and children until the time seems more propitious. That tends to be in their middle thirties. They then look round and find that many of the once 'eligible' men are already married or do not want a 'commitment'.

WHERE ARE ALL THE SINGLE MEN?

Where do these partnerless 30+ women now find an eligible *single* man under forty – or even stretching the age gap a bit, under 50? The problem is felt especially by women wanting to have children, for pregnancy gets less likely as they approach the menopause, whereas men can go on having children until very late in life. Surrogacy is fraught with emotional hazards. Having a baby is possible by impregnation with donor sperm, but this option is usually favoured only by a woman desperate to bear a child. She may be prepared to become pregnant by an invisible father, a man never seen, and who has never shown her love. What of children born in this way? How will they feel having a father who does not care whether they live or die?

The facts

The dearth of eligible males for women in their thirties is more apparent than real. In the UK there are actually more younger men than younger women. For the whole of the 20th century more boys than girls have been born: 104 boys to every 100 girls. In developing countries this ratio remains as in the world as a whole, but more girls than boys die between one and four years of age. Although the figures for male and female births tend to be similar throughout the world, there are occasional variations for which no explanation can be found. As an example, the proportion of boys increased briefly during and immediately after World War One. The numbers rose again in the early thirties to just over 105 per 100 female births. Another marked increase occurred around the middle of World War Two.

After the early forties, there was a 40-year period of stability in relative birth rates during which time around 106 boys were born for every 100 girls. In the eighties fewer boys were born. The statistics now continue to show around 105 male per 100 female births. This higher ratio of males to females is maintained but with the preponderance of males reducing until in the UK, numbers of males and females in the 45 to 50 age group is roughly the same. After this plateau the proportion of males in the population drops considerably.

Other influences affect these trends. In the UK as in other industrialised countries the death rate is higher for young boys than for girls of the same age. In developing countries the reverse is true but this inbalance is being remedied by fewer women in those countries dying in childbirth. The number of men dying between the ages of 29 and 40 years in the UK, however, is currently at its highest for a century. The Department of Social Statistics reported in 1996 that young men were dying at this early age because of the new danger of AIDS and the stress of modern living, including the trauma of divorce or separation. Men apparently adapt less well than women to a life alone and commit suicide more frequently. Women also live longer than men. The early surplus of males to females caused by more boys being born than girls thus levels out and later reverses. After the age of 50, in almost all industrialised countries, more women survive than men.

The 'surplus' of men to women in the teens and twenties means that at those ages, women have a wide choice of partners. When a partnership comes to grief within the first five years, they can take their leave and graze in richer pastures elsewhere. In the older age groups from 40 to 50 onwards, it is men who have more choices. Even if they are already 'committed' or 'promised' as they would say in Ireland, they may be tempted to look around at what's on offer, and unfortunately, for those left behind, there is usually plenty.

MAN: THE ENDANGERED SPECIES?

Along with changes in population and the economic position of women over the last decades, there has been an almost unnoticed change in the status of men. This used to come from power, inherited or created by the man himself. In the middle and upper classes that power meant titles, money and position. According to Rosalie Osias of *The Los Angeles Times*, 'the man with the biggest club still gets the woman'. She once wrote of President Clinton that he 'exudes so much power and charisma that women were willing to ignore domestic flaws in the White House that would detonate a divorce in their own homes'. A survey of 800 female secretaries by her own research institute showed that 68% of them found power and position to be one of a man's most sexually attractive attributes.

Muscle-power

For working class men in the UK and doubtless in other countries too, power used to be rated in terms of their physical strength. Men and women may be equal in courage, endurance and brainpower, but men are taller, stronger and bigger. They have a longer reach, more powerful muscles and usually a far more compelling sex drive. They can walk, run and swim faster than women.

In the early part of the twentieth century, when unemployment in the UK hovered round the two million mark, the strongest man capable of hard manual labour was one of the 'lucky' ones. He was, for example, able to push his way to the front of a throng of 600 men scrambling for one of the 20 jobs available at the London docks. For the 'privilege' of getting this work, he earned all of sixpence an hour with the chance of drowning or other accident and no compensation. Without that meagre wage, however, his family could end in the workhouse. The welfare state was not yet born.

A working class wife might earn a few shillings by cleaning, washing, sticking boxes together, making streamers, basting trousers or other forms of usually sweated labour, but her husband was the main earner: the breadwinner. His earnings were all-important for the family's survival. If food was short, he had to be given the main share to keep up the strength needed for his job. Even when he was not an unskilled manual worker but a tradesman, his earnings, not those of his wife, determined the quality of life which the family had.

THE NEW BALANCE OF POWER

Technology changed that picture. It lessened the need for physical strength. Those who provided manual labour – young and old, the hewers of wood and the drawers of water – were no longer essential in a modern economy. That should have released them from the daily grind of providing for a family by gruelling work for long hours in factories and underground for a pittance. However, with technology, super-women and lesser varieties of the species appeared on the scene. Their contribution to the household income was no longer derived, like that of their mothers and grandmothers, from part-time virtual slavery at home. It might now be almost as much as and sometimes more than their partners. This apparent equality has proved elusive for both sexes. Juggling careers with the needs of children and home sometimes proved a bit too much of a good thing, even for superwomen.

But the position of men as breadwinners had already been demoted. They are no longer seen, if seen at all, as the head of the family but downgraded to sperm providers and pleasure givers. Healthy young men, like pedigree bulls, can now be valued and paid for their ability to reproduce. Why do they allow themselves to be used in this way, to help breed children they will never know or see? Can it really be for the love of their species? Have they got a super ego complex? Or are they just after the money?

A young sperm donor writing in *The Independent Review* (Monday 26 January 2004) gave one answer. As a young student in 1982, he was always hard up. (What student isn't?) Being as he thought and maybe was, a bit brighter than his fellows, he decided to forego earning a bit of extra cash by the usual route of bar tender, cleaner, store packer and so on, and turned up at a hospital which, he discovered, paid sperm donors £5 per attendance. On his first visit he was greeted like a philanthropist and having proved himself, the ritual of his golden contribution was thereafter kept secret and unobtrusive.

Unwisely mentioning this part-time 'job' to an envious friend (a fiver was not so easily come by in those days), he was thereafter ragged by his fellows for the rest of his student days. They loved telling him that they had seen in the high street a baby/child that looked like his spitting image. Was he the father? His friends who lacked his entrepreneurial spirit took it all as a great joke. Much later, after a few more ejaculations in London at £15 a time, he heard that the UK government was considering a new law to give children of sperm donors the right to know the identity of their father. He had visions of endless children turning up on his doorstep claiming to be his sons or daughters. The new bill was not retrospective and he was therefore spared this fate (though another now gives fathers named on a child's birth certificate after 1 December 2003 automatic parental responsibility for such children).

The prospect of such a law and a TV programme featuring men and women who had been fathered by sperm donation made this donor think doubly hard about the whole process in which he had taken part. The 'fatherless' men and women he saw on TV felt betrayed, angry and isolated. Unlike adopted children who can at least search for their parents, there was no hope for those created by an anonymous donor of finding who was partly responsible for their birth. They had almost no chance of ever tracing their father and finding out about some part of their genetic heritage.

CHILDREN NEED FATHERS

Being a parent is more than being a sperm or egg provider. Procreation is usually pleasurable and sometimes, at least according to all the best romances, ecstatically so. If it were not, far fewer children would be born. But that is only the beginning. Some single mothers often do a wonderful job bringing up their daughters and create with them a powerful, long-lasting relationship. Young lads are more influenced by 'achievers' whom they can emulate. They tend to take notice of authority laid down by someone more powerful and physically bigger than themselves.

The lack of a father figure, a prototype on which they normally base their own ideas of male adulthood, can make them feel alienated. This absence, whether because of divorce, a moment of passion and a hasty exit thereafter, a sperm injection from an unknown donor, or in the case of the very young, curiosity, has the same result. In the place of fathers never seen, known or spoken of by mothers with respect or love, boys substitute football 'heroes' or the gunslinging characters with a vocabulary of four words and not much else, seen on TV and in American films. The example of other 'heroes' is sometimes worse.

Consequences of having no father figure

The majority of crimes against the person, of mugging and burglary, are committed today by young males, usually from homes where the father is missing or unknown. Research by Professor Kathleen Kiernan of the Social Policy Unit (London School of Economics) reveals some grim figures about children from fatherless families. They are:

- 8 times more likely to be murdered
- 18 times more likely to murder
- 40 times more likely to fail in the education system
- 20 times more likely to be unemployed
- 32 times more likely to be homeless
- 10 times more likely to abuse drink and/or drugs
- 35 times more likely to be in prison.

Professor Kiernan blames unmarried parenthood for these 'fragile beginnings', yet further research shows that children of lone father families develop similarly to those in two-parent households. It is the absence of fathers as role models that appears to harm children.

Stepfathers do not necessarily feel affection for another man's teenage son living in the same house. A stepdaughter may get unwanted attention. Teenage sons, for their part, do not always become as endeared to step-siblings or their mother's new lover/husband as she is. Such emotions can lead to friction in the home and homelessness in the streets. Sons and daughters need a good father as a role model of men generally, otherwise their own future happiness may falter, even if it does not follow the same pattern as that of their separated/divorced parents.

In the case of boys, rejection, as they see it, can lead to heartbreak or violence; in daughters, guilt, distress and emotional instability. Yet even devoted fathers are finding it more and more difficult to keep in touch with their children after a divorce; 50% of them lose contact altogether within three years. This may be due to:

- the attitude of the mother
- her new partner
- financial difficulties
- commuting problems.

However much he loves his children, and for many it is a most terrible blow to have to lose them, even temporarily, the father tends to lose contact with them over time. Unless he is very highly motivated or a legacy or heritage is involved, he gradually becomes exhausted with the effort of trying to keep in touch with his children and finally gives up seeing them at all.

Family law in the UK is heavily weighted against the father having custody and can cause him and his children great grief. Bob Geldof wrote a brilliant and moving plea in *The Times* 5 December 2003, describing the tribulation of divorced men such as himself trying to keep in touch with their children.

MARITAL HARMONY

A study by the National Association for the Care and Resettlement of Offenders (NACRO) found that children in trouble with the police have little or no attachment to their fathers, even if they still live at home. Where the father never joined in the activities of their children at the age of 12, for example, this doubled the risk that the youngsters would be convicted of a crime as teenagers and of violent offences later in life.

From research in several countries, NACRO found that twice as many boys offended whose fathers had left home because of marital breakdown as those whose parents lived together in relative harmony. Delinquency was far more often associated with fathers being absent because of 'parental conflict' than with fathers being absent through death or illness. Children under four when their fathers left were most likely to go on to serious crime. One study found that a third of working class boys whose parents were separated through marital breakdown were convicted as juveniles, and girls are currently fast catching up with boys in terms of violence.

Marriages arranged by 'brokers' similar to the Jewish *shadchen* may be the answer to marital harmony. One *shadchen* is reported to have told his client Izzy that he knew of a beautiful woman who would just suit him. The very modern Izzy replied, 'Tell her that as a good businessman I like to sample goods before I buy them.' The *shadchen* did as he was bidden and came back with the message, 'Hetty says she is good at business too. She doesn't give samples, but has lots of references.'

Why bother?

In modern marriage, no matter what vows are taken, neither partner can rely on a lifetime's commitment by the other. The wife can divorce the man, get custody of the children and retain the family home. The husband is shoved out, sometimes so that his wife's lover can move in. This is perhaps an exaggerated picture of the hazards of marriage for the modern man but it is enough to put many young men off that idea altogether. What do they lose by foregoing marriage and 'shacking up' with a woman, instead? And if the woman is happy to go along with this attitude, what has she got to lose? If she becomes pregnant, he can move off and leave the state to pick up the bill. Indeed a teenage girl might find that being a young single mother housed by the council and fed by social security has more to recommend it than living in the parental home tied to an unemployed loafer lounging around the house or drinking down at the pub.

'Cast off' older wives

For older wives the scenarios are different – though sometimes worse. After perhaps 15 years or more of working in the home, looking after children, accompanying husbands on prestige raising trips abroad, acting as unpaid secretaries, or giving up a career for less well paid or part-time jobs, they can easily be discarded for younger models. They may not be so nubile as they once were, and unlike men of the same age, usually have less opportunity, if they should so want, of another partner. Lacking a skill, the poorer among them may also find it hard to get work and have to take a low wage job to make ends meet. Pension rights once expected and assets such as the family house might be in jeopardy and along with companionship and a once comfortable lifestyle, go up in smoke.

Wives who have been 'cast off', through no discernible fault of their own except that of growing older, often become more cynical about men than they used to be and so team up with somebody unsuitable. In spite of working harder this time because, misquoting Wilde, 'to divorce one partner looks like a misfortune, to divorce two looks like carelessness', the next few years at least could see a bumpy ride for them and yet another applicant for the ever growing First (and second and third?) Wives' Club.

When you grow tired of somebody, today's message is to move on. Ignore any promises you made in the registry office, or at the altar. You have your own life to live. Think above all else of your own needs, your own happiness. Ignore the rest.

The cult of celebrity

The many spouses and lovers of rich people or 'celebs' are written about as if everybody, not only those intimately involved, gains more happiness from this inconstancy. Newspaper inches give them valuable publicity – hard luck on discarded pawns in these games of sexual chess. Get yourself a better agent. Young children, older wives or lovers, are the ones who most often lose out financially, physically or emotionally.

Most important from a social point of view is that trend setters like these 'celebs' encourage those who have neither the opportunity nor the money to copy their example. Imagining such a lifestyle is worth striving for, they forget that short-term marriages or pairings give short-term happiness. Partnership is meant for the long term. Like a financial investment it does not soar ever upwards. It goes through troughs and peaks, yielding gains and dividends on the way. With a bit of luck thrown in for good measure, it is always possible, **if you know**

yourself and what you want, to meet somebody whose company you enjoy so much you will want to live with them, not for a night and a day, but for at least part of a lifetime.

The following chapters will help you to discover more about yourself while or even before you start looking for a counterpart on either side of the gender line. They also suggest other options that you may never have considered, but which could give you more happiness and peace of mind than chasing after an elusive Will or Willa of the wisp.

3

Hitched or Ditched? The Fear of Commitment

Sister Mary Joseph finished, rather wearily, her religious lesson for the top class, on the sacrament of marriage. They were the oldest though not the brightest group in St. Anne's School, but in Sister Mary Joseph's breast, hope never died.

'Tell me one of the conditions for a marriage to be legally valid,' she asked them. Somebody would surely answer, 'over sixteen' or 'voluntary' or one of the other conditions she had mentioned in the past 30 minutes.

Ginger haired Rosie sitting at the back of the class did not hesitate. She put up her hand. 'Yes, Rosie. What is necessary for a valid marriage?'

'Please, sister,' replied Rosie, 'A feller.'

Rosie, whose looks meant she would never be short of a 'feller', had put her finger on one of the basics of a marriage contract. Ignoring for the moment the idea of same sex partnerships, there must be two parties to a marriage contract: a man and a woman. If either bride or groom fails to turn up, the wedding can't take place and the day is unlikely to be a rousing success. It may turn out to be a memorable one, but for all the wrong reasons. And though you can insure against all manner of contingencies affecting the BIG DAY, even the destruction of the wedding veil by the spitting image of Mr. Rochester's first wife, you can't insure against a bride or groom deciding not to appear.

Neither can you insure against either of them turning out to be Mr. or Mrs. Hyde after the wedding instead of the Mr. or Mrs. Jekyll they were before. This might be why your past 'romances' have ended in failure. Perhaps you choose or allow yourself to be chosen by somebody who is never going to give you any commitment. And the reason for those choices is that it is you yourself who is afraid of it.

A WEDDING OR MARRIAGE?

Girls, for example, are often caught up in the excitement of other women's engagements, the handsome man whose love they have won for ever, his ring (holding out a finger for closer inspection), the wedding arrangements, magazines, the number of guests and bridesmaids, their dresses, and all the other paraphernalia that go to make up most modern weddings. They are further enchanted by the glitter and the glitz, not to mention the cost, of many celebrity marriages. Never mind that these may last only a few months… in one famous case less than 20 hours. Magazines battle to get pictures of the bride, the groom, their wonderful attire and wedding breakfast (but, unless they want to risk being sued, never of anybody actually eating it) and no mention of the fee paid for this 'free' publicity.

Such pictures along with chat in offices and factories, often act as a subtle inducement for girls to tie the knot with their current boyfriend, however unsuitable he might be as a long-term partner. They do not even seem to contemplate the future life they will lead together, except perhaps in material terms. The marriage lasts a few years, if that, and a breakup follows, often with emotional upsets that last a long time afterwards. Yet this conclusion could be seen almost from the start. The package not the contents were the attraction. Once the package has been discarded, the contents soon follow.

MORE THAN PHYSICAL?

Men get caught up in another type of trauma. The package in this case is a woman's beauty, her charm, sometimes her 'fatal attraction'. Even if the man realises she is unsuitable in other ways, somehow he finds himself, against all his more rational judgement, desperately wanting more than friendship. Unlike women, he is blessed/cursed with an organ which when functioning does not allow him to use his brain. For her part, the girl is more than willing to be seduced into a relationship by protestations of love. Without making any commitment, the pair move into his or her place and before long wonder whatever caused them to do so. They will be lucky if they manage to split up without some emotional or financial damage – especially if she becomes pregnant.

That alters everything and for short-term relationships, rarely for the better. Save for a few odd instances we are long past the age of chivalry. Nearly half a decade has passed since Allan Sillitoe wrote in *Saturday Night And Sunday Morning* about the working class lad who gives up his aspirations for betterment to wed the local lass he has got 'into trouble'. The much more likely scenario today is for the man to leave the young mum or pregnant lover to the tender mercies of the local council and the Department of Social Security.

Relationships between young men and young women usually lead along either of two paths: (i) a breakup or (ii) setting up home together in marriage or outside it. Breakups depend on many things, sometimes quite small ones ... or so they seem to outsiders. Setting up home together does not include the non-sexual relationships, such as flat sharing. These are restricted from developing into anything more by constraints of kinship (family) or place (office, school, etc.) and can go on for years. By contrast a 'platonic' friendship, so called, between a man and woman, can continue only when one is unable to go further because of constraints of a different kind: legal, moral or physical.

Allowing for these exceptions, platonic 'friendships' are doomed to failure. They promise much, but deliver little, especially of commitment. And the reasons they deliver little might be because:

■ one of the pair does not want more
■ there is too big an age gap
■ a pseudo-kinship relationship (godfather, adopted 'uncle') exists
■ a fear of physical sex (it happens)
■ one, or both, are already married and unable to exchange one tie for another, though happy enough to take whatever is available.

Other reasons are that one of the pair prefers:

■ the company of their own gender or
■ non-physical communication, for example by letter.

The following examples show how commitment is avoided by always finding the wrong man or woman to pair up with.

Example 1: Avoiding commitment

Comment from a 36-year-old woman owner of small cafe:
'I used to think I wanted a committed man, but when I look at the kind of men I've fallen in love with, I realise that I'd be terrified if the right man really came along. The truth is I'm afraid of intimacy and that's probably why I'm always choosing the wrong guys.'

Example 2: Avoiding commitment

Comment from a 23-year-old secretary:
'Whenever I go out with a man, the affair, if you can call it that, lasts for about eight weeks, never longer. Then he seems to get frightened that he's going to be trapped into something more, and disappears. That's OK by me, because I don't want to settle down for another four or five years anyway. I probably choose the men I do, because they usually haven't got much to offer except looks. Still, if the right one came along, I might change my mind.'

Example 3: Avoiding commitment

John is 33, a good looking computer programmer. He loves challenges, in love and in work. Unfortunately for any girl who comes up against him, he loses interest in the romantic battle as soon as he appears to be winning it. So the girl who is apparently not attracted to him is the one he always seeks out. When, as is invariably the case, she starts to reciprocate his interest, she's lost him. To get closer she then tries out all the stratagems he has used on her. In vain. He has only been testing out his attractions on somebody who seems to be unaware of them. Once she has shown that she realises what a wonderful guy he is, he disappears for another conquest.

The only way to deal with this kind of non-committed person is to be equally non-committal yourself. No premarital sex here. You'll gain nothing by giving in. Similarly for gamblers, alcoholics, drug addicts and people already married whose wives/husbands don't understand them but who don't want a divorce.

THE LONG DISTANCE LOVER

'Pen friends', where two people communicate but rarely see each other, is one way of having a fairly long-term relationship without any commitment by either of the writers. These far distant 'affairs' are becoming more common. Working holiday visas issued to young visitors to the UK, student gap years and cheap air travel all bring people together from across the globe. Many inter-country/continent friendships result from such intermingling.

Usually they blossom for a while and then die a death. If face to face meetings do not proceed much further than letter writing or email/text messages, it is usually due to the fact that the parties do not want anything more. They prefer their present (single?) lifestyle. That is why they like being pen friends. Only the strongest of relationships can survive a long separation. New acquaintances of marriageable age need to see, touch and speak with each other to keep a relationship moving.

In long distance loving, the man is usually happy to keep the affair on a low key. The woman ostensibly seems to want more, but in truth she is often more afraid of commitment than he is. This is why, even if she sheds a few tears after their occasional corporeal interludes, the romance never proceeds beyond endearing, and occasionally passionate letters or emails.

If one of the duo really wants more than the occasional meeting up with each other, here are some useful do's and don'ts.

Do's and don'ts of long-distance relationships

Do	Don't
Be honest. let your friend know if you want something more than talk over the airwaves. How long are you prepared to wait for it? Time passes.	Move house or change jobs or make any other lifestyle alterations unless you have a positive commitment.
Send something more than an email occasionally.	Wait for the annual Valentine's Day or birthday to send a special message/parcel.
Make an arrangement to share any expenses.	Bear the sole costs of visits, phone calls.
Express your feelings more openly than you would face to face. You cannot get to know each other unless you do.	Give up mixing with other people, trying new places or feel guilty about enjoying them.
Break off when you have to, as firmly yet as sensitively as you can.	Continue with the relationship when you feel it has run its course.

Here is a true case of commitment, an extraordinary one of somebody who gave up letter writing for closer contact, ignoring, so it seemed, all the usual warnings.

Example 1: Unusual commitment

Maggie Simmonds, a 39-year-old widow with four children, wanted a little more excitement in her life – something to break the spell of her job as a hairdresser and the cooking and cleaning at home. One day she spotted an advert in a free newspaper asking if anybody would like to 'write to inmates in another country'. Maggie got in touch and was given three names. One of them was a murderer who had stabbed a 31-year-old single mother in the head and chest while the two of them were drinking beer and listening to CDs. Hardly the ideal acquaintance, one would think.

Nevertheless Maggie wrote to Dick Rampo, a reputed member of an American Indian tribe, telling him all about herself and receiving in return letters addressed initially to the newspaper, which thereby avoided giving inmates the addresses of correspondents. The friendship gathered pace. She filled in a visitor's application form sent to her by the prisoner, flew to Seattle, then to Washington State Reformatory 100 miles away, to meet him for the first time and to fill in a few more forms.

In spite of the difficulties of prison visiting (less stringent than in the UK), the pair got on very well. Before Maggie returned to Britain, she signed further papers to get permission for a prison wedding. After ringing her four children, all very enthusiastic about her news, she gave up her hairdressing job and sold every item she possessed including her house.

The family flew to the US, temporarily moved in with the new in-laws and the wedding took place shortly afterwards. Maggie was given by the prison authorities all the details of her husband's crime (he was apparently high on drugs at the time) and his possible release date. She declares that she has made a lifetime's commitment and will wait for him.

Nobody can deny that in this example, there certainly was commitment on both sides, though one appears to be gaining very much more from it than the other.

Example 2: Unusual commitment

Two young lawyers, both in their twenties, met and became interested in each other. The man was then transferred for two years to Papua New Guinea while the woman remained in Sydney. Though their relationship was very new when they parted, they knew they had something good going for them and they didn't want to lose it. He visited her every six weeks. They focused on the fact they wanted to marry and that they loved each other. They wrote long letters each week backed up by emails. Phone calls were stressful because they couldn't see the expression on the other person's face and had to deduce everything from the words spoken and the tone of voice.

The fact that they each had their own jobs and were not dependent on the other helped the relationship; so did the fact that the man in this case wore his heart on his sleeve, so giving his partner extra reassurance while he was away.

This long distance loving ended happily – that is not often the case. Psychologists declare that it is hard to maintain closeness when you are physically distant from each other. You need to have an aim and stick to it. If you want a short-term relationship, then long distance loving is not for you. And if you can't resist the temptation of those near who want to become dear, then close the relationship with the man or woman from afar.

A DIFFERENT LIFE

Example 3: Unusual commitment

Lucy Winkett, a 19-year-old Cambridge undergraduate, brilliant musician and singer, anticipated a glittering professional career and a lifetime with her boyfriend Andrew Stillwell. He was a few years older than she and they had met in their home county of Buckinghamshire before both went up to university. After graduating and while waiting to begin an accountancy job, Andrew took a walking holiday in the French Alps with some friends. It was his last. He slipped, fell down to the rocks below and died a week later in a Geneva hospital with Lucy and his family by his bedside. For a young girl in the middle of a degree course it was a devastating blow. She graduated, but the helplessness she had felt in the face of death led her on to a new path, the desire to become a priest.

At the age of 28, six months after her ordination, she was appointed as the first woman priest at St. Paul's Cathedral in London. After the death of a much loved sweetheart, other women might later have opted for a regular job, a man, a house and a car. These things no longer mattered to Lucy. She came to terms with Andrew's death, answered what she viewed as a new vocation, and started living again.

What kind of lifestyle are *you* seeking? Marriage or cohabiting is not the only option. There are others. Friendship with somebody of your own gender is one. In spite of what outsiders may think, it doesn't have to be a sexual one, but an arrangement that suits your financial or domestic situation. Lucy Winkett chose a religious vocation. So did Reverend Father Bryan Storey of Tintagel, Cornwall. When he was training 40

years ago, a priest told him that the greatest fulfilment in life was the Catholic priesthood. He finds those words equally true today. Spending many hours each week in prayer and meditation, he says, deepens faith, and keeping the celibate promise does 'untold good in days when so many marriage vows are broken.' According to geneticist David Gems of University College, London, using research based on the sex lives of nematod worms (!) a further advantage of celibacy is that it enables men to live longer, for they are not genetically programmed, he asserts, to live shorter lives than females.

REMAINING SINGLE

More negative reasons can cause men to remain single. Sometimes, as with a 48-year-old bachelor film producer, it is the result of the volatile marriage of parents and their subsequent separation. He has had lots of girlfriends but the divorces and resultant anguish of his friends has further put him off matrimony. Another single man of 41 doesn't want to be the oldest father in the street, but of the two relationships he has had, one broke up acrimoniously and the second girl could not make up her mind. Some men are uncertain of their sexuality and do not marry on that account but most men remain single either because of their career structure or because they haven't yet met the right person.

It is interesting to note, however, that according to John H. Laub and Robert J. Sampson, authors of *Shared Beginnings Divergent Lives*, marriage turns young male delinquents away from crime. Giving the results of interviews with former young criminals to find out what if anything induced them to turn away from crime, Laub discovered three factors: a spell in the Armed Forces, a steady job and marriage – and the most important was marriage. This report also suggests that marriage benefits men more than women, a conclusion emphasised in other reports.

SPINSTERS GIVE MRS A MISS

For women, the chance of a high flying career has given them the option of *choosing* to remain single. They assert that they can earn more money and have more fun being single than married. They have everything they want: a lovely home, good social life and great friends. By the time they get to that peak, however, they are in their 30s. They are then more 'choosy', not prepared to take on anybody just for a change of title. Most of the 'eligible' men have already been snapped up and even if single women do find the right person, they fear the relationship might not last, so they build up careers instead. Petronella Wyatt, writing in *The Daily Telegraph*, avers that there is no better alternative to marriage than work and that the pleasure you get from professional success is 'one of the greatest life has to offer'.

In Jane Austen's time (see Chapter 2) and indeed long afterwards, marriage was almost the only choice for women. Now they no longer rely on men for their support. Neither do they have to be weighed down under a burden of domestic trivia. (Read *Fear of Flying* by Susan Jongh for the story of an intelligent woman coping … and losing.)

Ask yourself if you want to be one of the modern women who are giving marriage a miss for careers that offer the chance of happiness, independence and fulfilment? Do you prefer to be hitched or rich? Think about the commitment you have to make. To what or to whom? It's your life, your destiny. If you enjoy your comfortable single life, stick with it rather than throw yourself away on some no good, no hoper. He will take up most of your time, much of your money, and maybe break your heart in the process. Don't forge links with somebody who promises to reform, to give up this, that or the other addiction, when he has so far shown neither the will, the desire nor the capacity to do so.

THINK YOU CAN CHANGE HIM?

Example: No change

Sam, a brilliant lecturer in accountancy, was also an expert at gardening and DIY. A good and lively companion, he seemed to outsiders an ideal husband. His wife knew differently. Sam had one big weakness – alcohol. Perhaps this was partly due to the fact that the couple had no children and Sam's wife was subject to fits of depression. His colleagues knew his situation and when he came in to lectures the worse for drink they tried covering up for him, using all manner of stratagems to keep the truth from students and hierarchy. In vain.

One evening he came in shouting and singing instead of lecturing, and nobody could quieten him down. He was called up the next day and severely cautioned by the head of department. A female lecturer who knew his wife and how she had struggled to 'reform' Sam, warned him about the possibility of losing his job.

'Don't you think,' Sam replied, 'that as an intelligent man I know that? Don't you think that if I really wanted to change, I would try some organisation that might help? You see,' he added with great perspicacity, 'It's not the knowledge, it's the will.'

Being drunk saved Sam from thinking. Until he learnt to adapt to the facts of his childlessness and his wife's depression, or the situation altered, his wife and colleagues would labour in vain to 'reform' him.

If you meet a similar person with an apparently intractable problem (drugs, alcohol, gambling, violence) and want the kind of lifestyle that goes with that person, go ahead. But don't imagine you will win the battle. Assume you won't and if by some miracle you or some helpful organisation actually do change your man or woman, think of this as an extraordinary bonus. (But will he or she then leave you nothing left to strive for?)

Rather than make such a choice, aim for safety. Never pair off with some man or woman with an apparently intractable problem because you think you can change them. Take them as they are or not at all. Bookmakers, who are a realistic crowd, would give your efforts not even an odds on chance of success. You will probably do better for yourself and others, including perhaps your loved one, by becoming a volunteer worker in one of the many charities crying out for someone like you. There will be no end to the people there that you can help. Some of them at least will reciprocate, and you won't then have the pain of being confronted with continual crises inside your own front door.

DEALING WITH NON-COMMITMENT

Signs of a man or woman afraid of commitment (cold feet syndrome)

They:

- are workaholics
- are too busy to pursue or be pursued
- need their 'space'
- have a history of broken romances
- never do the calling, or writing
- say they don't want commitment
- refuse to discuss a future together.

- If you do and they don't (or vice versa) want commitment, say so. You'll both then know where you stand. Repeat it often.
- Hope if you must, but don't fight for more.
- Know the score. If it looks as if you're losing out, back off.
- Give an ultimatum, but be prepared for the consequences.
- Get on with the next chapter of your life.

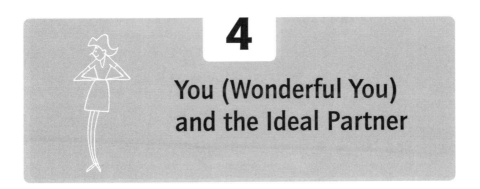

4

You (Wonderful You) and the Ideal Partner

WORKING AND WINNING

To achieve the aims you want, you usually have to work for them, but not always as the following story shows.

When a civil servant, known to have accumulated a huge income, retired to an expensive country house, several colleagues wanted to learn the secret of his extraordinary financial success. 'Playing the stock market?' they asked him. 'Tips, insider information, winning the Lottery, knowing a fraudster or two?'

He shook his head vigorously. 'Well how did you do it, then?' his listeners asked, anxious to discover how he had come by such great wealth. 'Hard work, hard work and more hard work,' he replied. 'And that's all. Just hard work?' His audience could not believe their ears. Why hadn't they been able to manage such a feat?

'Well,' continued the civil servant, anxious to avoid any misunderstanding, 'the million and a half my uncle left me in his will did help a bit.'

As the above story shows, achieving an aim does not come merely by working for it. Your aim in reading this book is presumably to achieve a happy long lasting relationship. But good or bad luck can play a part and make your aim difficult to achieve. You may be born in the wrong place at the wrong time. You or yours may have some physical impediment, incapacity or illness for which there are few palliatives and no cure and which you feel is not going to endear you to prospective partners.

WHAT YOU HAVE, YOU HOLD

When you cannot get what you want, however much you hope and work for it, relax, take stock. Assess what you have already gained or done. Look at all your successes, small though they seem. Give yourself a pat on the back for those achievements, however minor. Your life is not over yet, though it may feel like it – and who knows what the future holds? Perhaps you can change your lifestyle, alter your daily routine, take up a new hobby, or even exercise a bit for greater fitness, health and a more optimistic outlook?

If you are suffering from stress or pain caused by meeting the wrong person or parting from what seemed the right one, maybe you can use your experience to help others in the same boat. Diana, Princess of Wales, made what eventually proved an unfortunate marriage, but using her style, grace and beauty, used the platform provided by that marriage to do the good works that endeared her to millions. Nobody could have seen her funeral without realising how her life had touched people all over the globe.

In the final analysis, what cannot be cured must be endured. For the moment console yourself with the old adage, that where there's life, there's hope.

Good looks sometimes help the possessor to find the right partner, but not always. The unsophisticated possessor of good looks is sometimes unaware of the effect he or she has on others and so can be led into dangerous byways closed to the less well endowed. Success in marriage (by which I mean a lifelong partnership that provides mutual love and help, and more gladness than sadness) rarely depends on good looks. People who are not particularly good looking or who are physically or mentally disadvantaged need love as much as the fit and handsome and can maybe give even more.

Example 1: An impairment is no handicap to love

Shortly after David Helfgott, the gifted Australian pianist, won a gold medal at London's Royal College of Music, he temporarily lost his battle with manic hysteria, had a mental breakdown at 22 and for nearly 30 years was constantly in and out of psychiatric hospitals. In spite of his terrible affliction, which has not gone, and which can only be understood by those who have lived with it, he found a loving wife, returned to playing the piano and has since given public performances, including one in 1997 at London's Royal Festival Hall. His moving and triumphant story was told in the Oscar-winning film *Shine*.

Example 2: An impairment is no handicap to love

Former marine Chris Moon lost his right arm and leg in a land mine explosion while working with a charity in Mozambique, but never doubted that he would find a woman to love him. Six months after his accident he married. 'I would never want to share my life with someone who was interested in the outside of a person rather than the inside,' he said. 'Disabilities can't change you ... they exaggerate what you already are, for better or worse ... we all choose our own destiny and anything is possible. The only limits are what we lay down for ourselves.'

Wearing a false leg with shock absorbers on the knee, he was one of 350 competitors taking part in the Marathon des Sables, a slog across 144 miles of the Sahara desert in temperatures often reaching 100°F. Placed 283rd in the event, he said it was the hardest thing he had ever done. He wanted to show that disability can be beaten. 'Failure was never an option,' he said, but had to tell himself to keep going or just die.

MARRIAGE IS A MARATHON, NOT A SPRINT

Success in marriage is like running a marathon. It needs effort and the will to survive the distance. No runner wants to have DNF ('did not finish') recorded against his entry for any event. Divorce or the breaking up of a partnership is in effect a DNF marking.

Some marriages and relationships are doomed to a DNF finale right from the beginning. They are made too hastily, or when a couple are too passionately embroiled to consider the longer term consequences of their actions. When partners in a relationship don't stay the course it is usually because if things get difficult, as they always do, it's easier to get out than stay put.

Another reason for a marital break-up in today's climate is that one of the two parties may disappear and never be seen again. Most DNF cases, however, are due to disagreements which mount up over apparently trivial incidents. Other than those resulting from violence, these can usually be overcome or sorted out if the desire to do so is there. And with the right partners, they will be. So, assuming your aim is to be one of a couple, rather than a 'single', and you are looking for a partner rather than a friend, you have to find first of all, the 'right' person. And that generally means a spouse, for though you may dally on the way to the altar, marriage is invariably the best option if children are planned. More about marriage versus cohabiting is to be found in Chapter 9.

UNEQUAL EQUALS

Discovering the best partner does not come by sampling, except in a friendly way, everything on offer. Having too much choice of anything makes the decision harder not easier. Sexually experimenting with one man or woman and then another is likely to hurt somebody at some time. It may be you, if not today, tomorrow. Whatever is said or written about equality, it does not apply in the sexual sphere. The existence of prostitution through the ages is proof enough. The sexual organs of men and women are primarily meant for reproduction, but they also provide pleasure and relief – sometimes to such a degree that the primary purpose becomes a secondary one, or forgotten altogether.

A man tends to be driven by different and usually stronger impulses than those a woman feels. She normally functions more happily when she feels not only desired but loved, so it makes sense for her to avoid one night stands. If she chooses not to wait for marriage to experience sex, at least she wants to get some commitment, expression of affection or respect. Without love, you hover in the region of lust where desire overcomes all other feelings ... including common sense. It causes at best, recrimination, jealousy and guilt; at worst mayhem, violence and – occasionally – murder. Yet if sex weren't enjoyable, and passionately so, the human race would die out.

Nowadays men must tread far more warily. There are minefields out there, and not only from AIDS. A charge of sexual harassment, or worse, lies in wait for a man who does not respect a woman's right to say no. Rejections, partings or break-ups are equally unpleasant, even traumatic, for both men and women. Either may take revenge in ways that cause physical, mental or financial distress to themselves and others.

FIRM PARTNERS

Unmarried partnerships sound a sensible compromise. But they lack the structure, legal basis and united aim that has to operate in a business partnership if it is to succeed. In a sexual relationship, this united aim is often lacking and one or other of the partners proves vulnerable to take-over bids by predators. A few good partnerships provide a better home for children than poor marriages do. Most, however, are generally less secure while they last and statistically last a shorter time. Research suggests that living together before marriage 'to see how it works out' tends to increase the chance of divorce because the partners are less committed to the idea of marriage – the ease of release is one of the reasons why they cohabit in the first place.

The right partner is not always going to be somebody with whom you fall head over heels in love the first time you set eyes on one another. If that happens, treat it as a gift from the gods and pray that it will survive the next few months. Marriage is a long-term arrangement, the most convenient one so far devised, for the teamwork expression of love, passion, friendship, respect and especially for the bringing up of children in a safe and loving environment. If you crave a man or woman for sexual pleasure and nothing else, this book is not for you. There are plenty of better sources of information.

MAKING THE BEST OF YOURSELF

Don't put any lack of success in finding the right partner down to your (often imagined) lack of physical attractiveness, etc. Give yourself a sporting chance of finding the right lifelong partner by making the most of the many gifts nature has given you. Perfect them. Boost your confidence and self esteem. Go on an ego trip. If you don't like the picture you see of yourself in the mirror, think how you can alter that picture without running to the nearest plastic surgeon. Minor adjustments can often make a big difference. Grey hair can be coloured; traces of facial hair on women removed. When you meet a new acquaintance for the first time, present the best image you can devise to fit the place or the occasion. A good outfit is no extravagance for an older woman. Emphasise the good things you have, and try to cure the bad – doctors or chemists may have the answer. Dress down for a casual meeting, up for something more formal.

INITIAL ATTRACTION

Ask yourself what first attracts one person to another? Sometimes it seems to be a mysterious alchemy or charisma that defies understanding. At other times it can be put down to something specific: good grooming, elegant walk, athleticism, translucent skin, lovely smile, voice, eyes, mouth, a beautiful head of hair, nice legs, ankles or other parts of the anatomy, youth, power, a good presence. Money certainly plays a part in attracting the good and the bad, especially the bad, but with a first meeting you usually don't know who is rich and who isn't unless you've previously scanned the Rich List. If you've got as far as that, your best advice is not to marry for money, but marry where money is.

Remember the senses other than sight, that stimulate: smell, hearing, touch. When you are introduced to somebody you find attractive, there's no harm in making the handshake last a little longer than would be the case in a more formal setting or whispering some sweet nothing when greeting somebody with an introductory kiss … or two. If things go well, you might try to be a little more daring later on. Don't be too eager. Make haste slowly. You don't have to play hard to get, but don't make yourself too easily accessible either; the fun is sometimes in the hunt.

CHASED

Olivia Williams, a 28-year-old unknown English actress, was sent by her agent to a seedy casting room in Soho. 'Angry and humiliated' by the poor audition, she turned down the part. Unknown to her, it was for a role in Kevin Costner's film, *The Postman*. Two weeks later he recalled her with a first class fare to Los Angeles. 'He said it was something to do with my smile,' Olivia reported.

Hold on to the fact that you are worth knowing (let's hope you are) and your company is worth cultivating. **Don't**:

- look back negatively at what has gone before – you can't alter it
- join organisations where you can't mix easily with other members.

Love can overcome the barriers of culture, religion, class and race and melt them away, but not always immediately.

I once knew a couple living abroad, in which the English woman always referred to her husband as 'that crooked Swiss'. Fortunately the words were accompanied with smiles and looks of such mutual affection that one could understand why, in spite of this constant 'insult' as it seemed to outsiders, this mixed nationality couple had lived together so happily for 30 years.

Similar examples are all round us. Love like this which bypasses national or cultural boundaries usually takes time to develop – but not always, as the following example shows.

Example 1: Crossing the cultural divide

On a study trip with her father to study climatic conditions in northern Canada, Edinburgh University zoology student Jo Matthews met Mark Alaqu and received the traditional Inuit greeting of rubbing noses together. After returning to her studies she longed to be with Mark. Her father continued his expedition with a colleague. Violent storms smashed their canoe. They became trapped in a fjord and had run out of food when Fate in the person of Mark intervened. Arriving in his canoe, he plucked the men from the rocks to safety, and 'saved our lives', said Dr. Matthews. When his daughter heard of the rescue, it confirmed her feelings for Mark. She collected her belongings and went back to Canada to marry him. With a son of the marriage, she then settled in a community of 1,000 people near Hudson Bay, made clothes from animal skins and hunted for her supper. Helped perhaps by the fact that her home has central heating to combat temperatures of −40°C, she has no regrets.

The religious divide is usually more difficult to cross than a racial/national one. Imran Khan and Jemima Goldsmith failed after a nine-year stint, but it can be done.

Example 2: Crossing the religious divide

Modern Times, a programme shown on British television, gave us the picture of a Jewish wedding full of the usual glitz and *chutzpah*. The extraordinary thing about this wedding, however, was that the groom, Steve, was a Christian. To marry Michaela his Jewish bride, he had to agree to be circumcised, take lessons in Hebrew and face a Jewish 'court' to show that he knew his lessons. He also had to adopt (which for many men might be the breaking point) Jewish dietary laws – no bacon for example. He did all these things not only with panache, but with good humour, grace and a generosity of spirit wonderful to behold.

LOVE AT LAST SIGHT

In spite of what is written in romantic fiction about love at first sight (although it does sometimes happen), it is really love at last sight you ought to be dreaming about. True love has to survive the test of living together for the unforeseeable future. Choose places where you are likely to meet people whose outlook is broadly similar to your own. The more events and places you visit, the more acquaintances you meet, the greater the chance of finding somebody with interests like your own. Opposites attract, but they can attract negatively. If you like classical music, you won't find like-minded fans in a jazz session. If you're fond of gentle walks, you're unlikely to meet a 'rambling' soulmate in a top flight athletic club where everybody is concentrating on winning the next Olympics (and that's presuming they'll let you into the club without first checking your athletic record).

Don't let the positive fact that you are unique turn into a negative. Groucho Marx famously said he didn't 'care to belong to any club that will accept me as a member.' He could afford to make jokes like this, it earned him a fortune. You're not in the same position. Such thinking won't get you very far. If you've made up your mind to change your present situation from being single to being one of a couple, you're aiming to get somewhere with somebody. In that case you will do better by remembering what the Australian Prime Minister Robert Menzies

said when accused by a Member of Parliament of harbouring a superiority complex: 'Considering the company I keep in this place, that's hardly surprising.'

NEUTRAL TERRITORY

As mentioned previously, 'platonic' friendships are possible between men and women only when certain restraints prevent those friendships developing further. Many of these restraints operate in the places where people meet. Those who want to can usually find ways of getting round the restrictions. Romantic literature and films are full of such examples. Otherwise, when you meet people in a neutral situation, neither of you is promising or offering anything to the other. Such neutral places include premises where you work (factories, offices, shops); study (universities, colleges, evening classes, libraries, training courses, investment seminars); wait (queues for proms, bus, theatres, Harrods sale, hospitals); holiday (beaches, hotels, planes, coaches); exercise (athletics, jogging, swimming, judo, cycling, polo, riding, orienteering, etc.); worship (churches, synagogues, temples); or volunteer (community activities, political associations and charities).

The best, though not the only way to find an elusive 'somebody' whose company you might enjoy and whose acquaintance you'd like to extend, is to meet lots of people on neutral territory such as some of those outlined above. Unless you have joined a dating agency or are answering a personal ad, don't set out with the deliberate aim of finding a partner. Hope if you must, but any sign of need will put off even casual acquaintances. Feeling trapped, they will back away.

NON-NEUTRAL TERRITORY

Organised 'singles' nights in pubs, libraries and other places are not neutral. You may inadvertently turn up at a supermarket on the night of a 'singles' meeting, merely because you've run out of pasta and couldn't do your shopping earlier. Your presence is likely to be misinterpreted. If you don't want to be chatted up, clear off. Otherwise don't clam up because some stranger of the opposite sex comments on the price of goods on the shelf or another equally boring topic. There's a difference between being neurotic and playing for safety. Luncheon or other types of fee paying clubs and organisations where the main object is to meet people of the opposite sex, similarly are also not entirely neutral.

Choose a group activity with care. Some 'neutral' groups are heavily weighted with more women than men or vice versa. So if you go on a strenuous sporting or adventurous holiday (unless it is very expensive) you will probably meet younger people and usually more men than women, whereas a bridge group is likely to have more older than younger members. An evening class in cookery or creative writing generally has more women than men while in a class in computer studies, motorbike maintenance, photography or chess, the reverse situation applies. If the subject is of more interest than the people you expect to meet, so much the better ... for the moment.

Join organisations and clubs for the enjoyment or knowledge they can give you, to expand your horizons, learn a new hobby, help the community or particular sections of it. Never join with unrealistic expectations of finding 'romance', though here again, while there's life there's hope, and as in all walks of life, luck sometimes plays a part.

Example 1: Luck finds a way

Emma Jacobs, daughter of disc jockey David Jacobs, decided she'd like piano lessons. When Emma visited her son Tom at his school Open Day, she saw his music teacher across the crowded school hall. She went up to him; they began chatting together and he agreed to teach her piano. After two or three lessons, he asked her out on a date. They were married 18 months later.

Example 2: Luck finds a way

Young fireman Richard Lightfoot and his girl friend Donna had split up and for two months had not seen or spoken to each other. Answering a 999 call at four o'clock one morning, Richard found himself in front of Donna's burning flat and smashed his way in to rescue her. Donna likened her rescue to the old Milk Tray advertisements (they usually featured some young fellow taking tremendous risks, scaling the heights or plumbing the depths to bring chocolates to his loved one). 'He was a real hero and saved my life,' said Donna, 'a bit like the Milk Tray man.'

Example 3: Luck finds a way

Minette was a Jewish lady who made a very unsuitable marriage at 18 and divorced a few years later. Returning to her native Paris from a touring holiday in Spain she was flagged down by two young men on a motorbike. Thinking there must be something wrong with her car, she opened the window to see what they wanted. One of the men grabbed her arm while the other stole her money from the car. She managed to borrow some cash from the local bank, but not enough for the return journey, and put a notice in the hostel where she stayed the night, to ask if anybody wanted to join her (pay half expenses) on the way back. A young Jewish man volunteered. They became friendly, married some time later, have two sons and have been married for more than 20 years.

Example 4: Luck finds a way

Lara Homberg and Anka Edlund met for the first time in a lift in Karlstad, Sweden. They did not know the lift would break down and they would have to spend the next 19 hours stuck there, before they were eventually rescued. The ordeal could not have been too bad, for afterwards they decided to marry. If you can spend 19 hours incarcerated in a lift with somebody and emerge unscathed, marriage to them should be a cinch.

Example 5: Luck (with a little help) finds a way

When the trauma of her divorce after 10 years of marriage had eased a little, Kay tried a dating agency. The five 'dates' proved so unsuitable that she gave up the quest for a new partner and turned instead to a new hobby. Seeing an advert for scene shifters and general dogsbodies in a local amateur dramatics society, she volunteered and was taken on. Joking about her dating experiences to Fiona, a young girl on the set, she learnt that Fiona's father was a widower. He sounded attractive ... and lonely. Fiona took Kay's phone number. The widower and divorcee met, and have been happily married ever since.

The above are all true stories where luck played a part in romance. Fate is not always that kindly. So after looking at your own strengths and weaknesses, what is the perfect way of finding the kind of man or woman who will be the right partner for you? You are spoilt for choice. There are any amount of supposedly foolproof answers. The only trouble with that is, as always, the bigger the choice, the harder the decision.

The average age for marriage in the UK is 28 for a woman and 30 for a man. You might retort that age is just a number. The higher it gets, the more valuable it becomes – a comforting thought when you reach the big digits still unmarried.

A NUMBERS GAME

Dr. Peter Todd of the Max Planck Institute in Munich is a man who deals in numbers and believes in their power to pluck the heart strings. Suggesting that you can find the love of your life through mathematics and that it does not have to be a long process, he uses the analogy of an employer interviewing job candidates. Once the employer has seen 37% of candidates, a picture of the ideal employee is built up and the next person to fulfil the criteria gets the job. Your choice of potential partner can be similarly made.

Unfortunately, the number of reasonably qualified candidates who apply for some jobs, such as journalism, is sometimes as many as 200 for one job. There is never going to be this ratio of potential partners seeking you out unless you are a Zuleika Dobson or an Errol Flynn, in which case you will have been snatched up already. The chance of meeting 12 possible partners seems remote, though yesterday's short stumpy boy can turn out to be the handsome muscled rugby player a decade later. More realistically, less than a handful is likely to have been the sum of your chances so far, and maybe they weren't such a wonderful handful at that.

By the time you have seen a dozen of the most attractive (you should be so lucky!) there are enough criteria to judge what you are looking for in a life partner and so you can safely take the next good one that comes along. On the other hand, as the best economists say, you can fall in love at a first meeting with somebody you hardly know, and with whom you discover you have almost nothing in common. And who can say a pairing of such unlikely souls is doomed to failure?

Another number crunching solution dreamed up by an American publishing executive, Susan Piver, is to ask your proposed partner 100 essential questions before you say I do. She suggests a time limit of 30 minutes to two days to focus on the questions in a quiet pre-arranged setting. As Bernard Shaw once pointed out, the Americans speak a very different language from the English. If they think that two people asking each other 100 questions is going to fuse them into a happy partnership, they've got another think coming.

The numbers game, however, won't easily go away. Leil Lowndes gives us 85 proven techniques for success ('based on scientific studies into the nature of romantic love') in her book *How To Make Anyone Fall In Love With You*. Highly readable American advice but sadly lacking any proofs of the techniques' effectiveness.

THE COMMON SENSE APPROACH

Numbers alone are not an infallible answer. Some are suggested in the next chapter. Meanwhile, you know the interests you have, the activities you enjoy, the principles you hold dear, the sort of looks that attract you (or don't), and the only way you can even *begin* to know whether a man or woman will suit you as a lifetime's partner is to go out with them a few times in fairly safe settings or communicate with them by letter, phone or the Internet. If you like what you see, read or hear, and have heeded the cautions set out in the next chapter, carry on. If not, and the difficulty, whatever it is, cannot be resolved, and there is no room for compromise, part with as much tact and grace as you can.

First appearances are important, but unless you are rich and famous, looks matter less (and money and security more) as you get older. Character and temperament are always important. When the looks are offputting, however, a first meeting may never proceed any further. Give new acquaintances the chance to blossom. You can try all manner of tests (graphology, colours, questionnaires, astrology, etc.) to see whether the person you have just met is going to be your Mr. or Ms. Right, but what may be right for you one year may appear to be wrong the next. Marriage needs courage as well as commitment.

Hope, but don't sit back and wait for luck or fate to help you. No matter what your age or situation is, there is nothing to stop you making the first move if you find someone you would like to see more often. What have you got to lose? Anybody who has the poor sense to reject you would not have made much of a partner anyway.

Example 1: Age is no barrier

John Bayley's first sight of novelist Dame Iris Murdoch was of her pedalling with difficulty on an old bike past the north Oxford college where he lived. It was a miserable day, and she looked deep in thought, cold and rather unhappy. Nonetheless the sound of Wagnerian trumpets seemed to reverberate in his ears and he could think of nothing but the absolute necessity of getting to know her as soon as possible. He found out that she was a philosophy don at the college next door, six years older than him and quite uninterested in getting married, least of all to him. Though still virtually a student, he somehow persuaded her. A wedding eventually took place and they were married for over 40 years.

Wagner seems also to have weaved a magical spell for Mrs. Jones, below.

Example 2: Age is no barrier

Mrs. Jones, a 63-year-old divorcee, joined an evening class to improve her knowledge of German and met there a bachelor of about her own age. She enjoyed his company and he seemed to enjoy hers also, but knowing he was a bachelor, she didn't rate highly her chances of developing a relationship. He made no move in that direction, and she wondered if and how she should. She decided to join him in the evening break time and 'chat him up' a little. If that went down well, she could then ask him out to coffee or a drink after the class. The worst that could happen was that one or other of them, the bachelor probably, would feel his 'space' being threatened and might leave that class and join another. Mrs. Jones made the move. He responded immediately. They are now meeting up for musical evenings, having discovered a joint interest in Wagner.

Example 3: Age is no barrier

Alan, a 25-year-old computer contractor, left London to take up a post in Ireland. He fell in love with the soft lilting voice (and many other attributes) of his lady supervisor. Though she was six years older than him and going out with the managing director of the firm, Alan sent her a Valentine card (good opportunity this) 'From an Unknown Admirer'. The supervisor soon discovered the identity and many other characteristics of her 'Unknown Admirer' and within six months of their first meeting, the two were married. They now have three children and have been happily married for nearly 20 years.

Example 4: Age is no barrier

Steve, taking a university degree, was fascinated not only by the accent of the French lecturer on his university course, but by her beautiful figure. At the end of her lectures he found it more and more necessary to stay behind, always for some good reason, such as seeking answers to questions absolutely vital for him to pass the course, or to say how much he enjoyed the lecture, how fascinating it was, etc. ... or anything else that he could dream up for a *tête à tête* with the object of his dreams. His French accent naturally took a remarkable turn for the better. So did the burgeoning love affair of the tutor and student, in spite of the difference in age and status. The only surprise when Steve finished the course was not that he ended it with the French lecturer for his bride, but that in spite of all his extra tuition, he managed to get only a lower second class degree.

Example 5: Age is no barrier

The convoluted yet simple plots Raymond Chandler wove in his crime novels were to some extent mirrored in his rather sad private life. When not writing, he was drinking, yet he remained a devoted husband to a woman he thought ten years his senior but who was actually more than 20 years older than he.

DARE TO BE BRAVE

If you meet anybody you really fancy, and they are unmarried or single, go for them. This may be difficult for both men and women in situations where certain taboos operate such as student/teacher, doctor/patient, manager/low grade employee. Making the first move has usually been a male preserve, but with the ever present threat of sexual harassment, it is a brave male executive who would make approaches to a female employee, a tutor to a student, or a male officer to an enlisted woman. For doctors and patients (unlike nurses and patients), the taboo is sensible. But there is no reason why in other situations, women should not pick up the gauntlet and make the first move towards a relationship. They have crossed most other boundary lines, and men might care to be absolved from a chore which they now find has threatening undertones. A certain amount of care and tact is needed, but it should not be beyond the wit of woman to show an interest in somebody and if there's no response to be able to return to the status quo.

At parties or similar gatherings it is easier to make an approach. So when you see a man whose looks appeal to you, use the opportunity to give him a nice smile, a quick darting glance, a flick of the hair. Come-ons like this have the advantage that men who respond to them think they have made the first move. If your efforts get no reaction, or not the one you want, hard luck. Say to yourself 'Next!' and look out for somebody more perceptive. When a person cannot appreciate your looks, your conversation, your physique, your generous nature and all the lovely traits of character you hope you have, hard luck again. It is they who've missed out. They don't deserve a person like you. Be thankful for your fortunate escape and move on to the next phase of your life.

Do not, however, look twice at a married man or woman, otherwise you may be responsible for breaking up a family. Many people seem not to care, and the excuses are always the same – something on the lines of 'they were breaking up long before I came along'. Of course the break up of a family by an interloper is common practice and we see the new family later, apparently happily married, but what of those left behind? Do they relish their displacement? What if you and perhaps your children were the ones left behind for a new 'love'?

SELF ANALYSIS

Below are some suggestions to help you analyse the type of partner that you feel would be right for you. The next chapter outlines venues and organisations where you might find this kindred spirit.

Type of person you are (tick as applicable)

shy modest	fun-loving	sporting athletic	intellectual	musical	religious	literary artistic

ACTIVITIES YOU ENJOY OR GROUPS YOU MIGHT LIKE TO JOIN

If they don't exist, start one! Find a church hall/pub/school room/library in which to meet, get yourself a treasurer and secretary. Organise coffee mornings, coach trips, theatre outings, guest speakers, tuition or whatever publicity helps the aims of the group.

The following are some activities which you can join ... or start:

Athletics, bowls, ballroom dancing, bridge, business, chess, cinema, computer games, cookery, cricket, darts, discussion groups (politics, religion, books, etc.), field studies, football, discos, eating out, gardening (allotment society), hill climbing, interior decorating, investment, orienteering, photography, polo, reading, shopping, skating, swimming, tennis, theatre, travel, voluntary work, visiting museums/castles/ancient monuments, walking, library reading and discussion groups often set up by the information department of the local public library.

Watching television has not been included as an activity because if you are watching the small screen, you are unlikely to watch or be watched by anybody else, and equally unlikely to talk or listen to anybody else. The break for adverts might offer the opportunity for communication, but you'll have to be quick.

Finally, steer clear of people or activities you think you would not enjoy. Unless duty is involved, there is no point in doing something you don't like just to please a person who makes no effort to please you.

5

Meeting Places and People

You've decided, after long deliberation about the single life, that in spite of its many attractions (freedom to do what you want, when you want, spend what you like on what you like, etc.), it is not for you. How then do you extend your circle of friends and possibly from among them find a marriage partner, even though marriage is not your highest priority at the moment? Having answered the questions at the end of the previous chapter, you know the type of person you are and the type you would like to meet. You also know what turns you off and the type of activity you enjoy. This should point you to the kind of person who might fill any void in your life. Now comes the hard part: where you can find them.

Men are rarely in a hurry to tie the knot unless it offers overwhelming attractions that can't be won in any other way. They know they have all their lives to choose the 'right' woman (sometimes several) with only one caution – the right woman might meanwhile be snapped up by somebody else.

By contrast, biology puts a constraint on a woman's choice. Being young is the best time physically for women to marry, but today's thinking is that it hinders career chances, so they delay marriage to get qualifications and better jobs and to improve their chances of a better lifestyle in the future.

You can meet people at any time, but the right age for marriage, for men or women, is when you are old enough to make sensible decisions about your aims and ambitions, and young enough to go for them. This philosophy does not fit in with current ideas.

Example: The right age for marriage?

Ask yourself what do Baroness David, Iris Murdoch and novelist Madeleine Wickham (aka Sophie Kinsella) have in common? The answer is that they all met their husbands at university. Iris Murdoch was not exactly in the first flush of youth when John Bayley saw her cycling along Oxford's cobbled streets and fell in love with her. And she was a Fellow, not a student. Novelist Madeleine Wickham, who met her fiancé at Oxford, defied convention by marrying when she was 21.

Madeleine Wickham says that marrying young does not have to be limiting. Marriage vows do not include any reference to housework or giving up your personal ambitions. You promise to love and cherish: a reciprocal arrangement that lasts forever and means that you can think long term. 'You have the freedom to gamble.'

START YOUNG, BY DEGREES

Getting into a university not only helps you to a bigger salary, with a loan big enough to lead you into bankruptcy, but most important of all, a choice of lifetime friends and partners. So the choice and number of A levels you achieve at school have a far wider impact on your future than the career you ultimately choose. They set you in a different circle of friends and acquaintances amongst whom may be your life partner. Beware. You need the right course or institution to come upon Mr. or Ms. Right. Though either or both *could* turn up at Dogsbody College or the University of Basham and Wallopem, older places of learning such as Oxford and Cambridge have the pick of what seems to be the best. Get there, and you will also have your pick of that year's crop.

Think twice

Choose your course with care. You could be accepted with rather poorer A levels for less 'popular' subjects like classics or theology or even chemistry. A much better academic record is needed when applying for history, English, law, PPE or similar sought after degrees. However, it is not easy to change direction once you are 'in' and you don't want to be turfed out in your first year because you cannot take root in your new environment.

Sometimes being 'disadvantaged' helps entry (postal code, inner city/ comprehensive/state education, physical handicap, etc.). Even then your application may not succeed unless your interviewer agrees with you that your brilliance and knowledge is quite exceptional. Sometimes a hobby with a big drop out rate such as parachuting, or a casual mention of all your community/charity work, will get you in when nothing else will.

St. Andrews tends to be favoured by Scottish nationals (why not?) and has been given a royal nod of approval by the attendance of a prince: an heir, second in line to the British throne, no less. Durham, Bristol, Warwick and Exeter are well thought of and Dublin gives an attractive Irish accent and sometimes a bit of drama to go with it. Trinity College, founded by Elizabeth I, and which did not accept Catholics as students for some 300 years, keeps the fascinating Book of Kells within its precinct (entrance fee required) and is a good hunting ground not only for books.

The better known universities and colleges in London (King's, LSE, Imperial, UCL, for example) have an international reputation. They offer all the amenities of London, but non-resident students often have to make long journeys from their homes for meetings and activities. These may be consequently less well attended than those in universities where there are more halls of residence. The two Colleges of Law in Holborn and Lancaster Gate suffer from the same difficulty, less apparent in their branches in the smaller towns of Guildford and Chester.

Landed gentry and other manors

The Cirencester Royal Agricultural College attracts a small coterie of landed gentry as well as students not entirely wedded to animal farms. So does Newcastle, newly enriched by an agricultural school. And there are many other colleges dotted all over the UK where you can study outdoor pursuits. While learning about agriculture, animal care, horse management and husbandry, you will certainly pick up a few useful tips about the human species.

If you have not wormed your way into any of the above places, try working for an invite to, say, a May Ball, or perhaps you could politely gate crash your way into a celebrity party. You could even add a title to your name. Alternatively you might be able to go to an American university, perhaps as a mature or post-graduate student, though you might have a four year wait. American universities seem to have more than their fair share of rich men, or perhaps it is the contrast with the poorer students that make them appear so. Harvard and Yale are difficult to assail, but Brown University, Rhode Island, costing some $42,000 for a two semester year, was the *alma mater* of the heir to the Fiat empire, Giovanni Agnelli, among other 'eligibles', and Georgetown University Washington is rumoured to have harboured a prince or two.

Computer buffs could think about Stanford in California, from which state Bill Gates of Microsoft and Hewlett Packard emerged. Fontainebleau near Paris is full of burgeoning tycoons. Its occasional scholarships enable the clever and needy to mix with the clever and rich. If you get there, don't reveal which group you belong to. It may change before the course ends.

Holiday jobs before or during your degree course help minimally, to pay your way through college and provide an opportunity to meet people and places you might otherwise never see. Cooking for ski parties is one way of landing in the white wastes of Val d'Isère, where the ratio of men to women is about three to one, and a girl can meet the most attractive huskies on two legs. These may be wobbly from drink, however, by the time she finishes her chores. Cooking for shooting parties offers an entrance into the glamorous if somewhat cooler world of the Scottish moors where you might bag a kilted laird if you sympathise deeply enough over his lack of luck with the birds, keep your eyes away from his legs and display, with due modesty, your own.

OTHER PROMISING SITUATIONS

But what if you missed or turned down the chance of a future spouse at the above places? You are now (long?) past 21 and looking elsewhere for friendship, romance, marriage. Where do you find it? Opportunity and hope wait out there. After your perusal of 'neutral' situations or places where neither of you is promising or offering anything to the other, try other channels.

Neutral places include evening classes and libraries; holiday locations: beaches, hotels, planes; coaches or clubs catering for those who want to try their hand (or other parts) at gym, athletics, swimming, judo, cycling, etc. More promising places might include turning up as a suitably accoutred spectator for a polo match. That introduces you to another world but will cost you dear. Nothing venture, nothing gain, and Camilla Parker Bowles is supposed to have first met the Prince of Wales at a polo match when he was still an eligible bachelor, so there are precedents. Democracy and fast living, however, is scything through the Western world at such a rate that the number of eligible princes and princesses gets fewer by the hour. A Danish prince managed to find a Tasmanian beauty to share his princely throne in spite of her reputed initial reluctance, while Spain showed the 'common touch' when Prince Felipe married a divorcée.

Orienteering, a combination of map reading and walking, appeals to what might be called the fit, intellectual walker or climber. It tends to attract more men than women. Other neutral meeting places include those for worship where sexes are not separated for prayer. Community activities such as political groups or charities also offer neutral meeting places for people of similar outlook. Older people can often find new friends at local bring and buy or craft sales. Methodist homes sometimes run sales of plants with a tiny entrance fee and a cup of coffee available. All the profits go to the running of the homes, so you can have your coffee, plump up your window box with suitable plants, find a convivial conversationalist and aid the homes – a case of all this and heaven, too.

WAIT FOR IT

Sometimes you can stumble across (not literally, though it could help) people like you (young, lively, cultured?) waiting in queues. Be choosy. Hospital waiting rooms are not quite the ideal places for chat, though they give you plenty of time for exchanging details of your hopefully interesting ailment or accident (a little imagination will not go amiss) and to show your caring, sympathetic nature. A Mills & Boon author could easily start a romance there.

Waiting at a bus stop with the rain pouring down in buckets is also not recommended unless you have the shelter of an umbrella to offer to some lonely, (attractive) fellow traveller. Find out where he or she is going so that (for safety's sake), you don't get off at the same stop. You can always arrange a second meeting on neutral territory (another bus stop?). If you're after a rich 'catch,' remember Brigid Brophy's aphorism that anybody who uses a bus after the age of 35 is a failure in life.

You might now say that about anybody over 25. Girls might also read Wendy Cope's clever little poem, 'Bloody Men'.

Good' queues, where there are plenty of lively minds (and bodies?) include those outside the Albert Hall (the Proms), Wimbledon (occasionally) for the tennis or Harrods for their January sale (avoid getting murdered in the crush). There is not normally a queue to enter the reference room of the British Library but once inside you can look up from the book you have borrowed for the occasion to eye the surroundings. Could there possibly be any lovely women or handsome men hovering over a text even duller than your own? More infrequent but much more promising are events like the funerals or anniversaries of public figures or other events. People come from all over the world to participate. To get a good viewing space, they are often prepared to bed down overnight on the pavement.

Such events, where space is so limited and there is such an atmosphere of camaraderie, are ideal occasions for meeting and making new friends. When Diana, Princess of Wales was laid to rest after her tragic death, the royal palaces were almost besieged by the multitudes. And there is nothing like two days' close proximity to another person, including possibly even sleeping on the adjoining bit of pavement, for learning as much about them as you would pick up in several months of meetings. Festivals of various kinds, where you wander around and discuss books or music or other interests dear to your heart, are also a good opportunity for commingling.

FIRST PAST THE POST

Racecourses are particularly happy places to visit. Forget Damon Runyon's stories of bets that came unstuck, Graham Greene's *Brighton Rock* and reprobate Jeffery Barnard's picture of the racing fraternity as consisting of stuck up trainers and snooty establishment people. Race courses today appear to operate a code of chivalry for ladies on their own. Social scientist Kate Fox, a director of the Social Issues Research Centre in Oxford, went to her first race meeting through a chance invitation but was so fascinated by what she saw that, funded by the British Horseracing Board (BHB) and the Tote, she wrote *The Racing Tribe*, a report of her 12 months' study into the body language and behaviour of the race crowds, part of which was published in the *Racing Post*.

Ms. Fox knew very little about racing before her chance invitation to Ascot and imagined it as elitist, dominated by touts and toffs. Once she got to the course, however, she became fascinated by the behaviour of the crowd, people making eye contact, smiling at each other and conversing with complete strangers. The only other area in Britain she knew like this where it was socially acceptable to talk to a complete stranger was at a pub's bar counter.

In her role of social scientist, she conversed with everybody, stewards and cleaners alike, and found the same behaviour patterns at all the race meetings she attended: sociability, relaxing of reserves and inhibitions along with strict conformity to the rules of racing etiquette, where everyone knows what is expected of them. Unwritten rules are (1) that you do not boast about any gains made (you should be so lucky!) so that however skilled you are at picking winners, you never mention them, and (2) you always joke about your losers even when you know creditors are somewhere waiting for you like hungry hyenas scenting a carcass.

Unlike the 'inquests' after a game of bridge, you forget and forgive all previous predictions and erroneous comments about the chances of the horses and jockeys after a race, and never refer to them again. This code of chivalry also says that all women are 'ladies' and must be treated with courtesy and respect. Chat up ettiquette is permissible, but excessive persistence is forbidden. In view of these findings it might be worthwhile taking a trip to one or two of the race meetings and having a bet – and who knows, you might win more than you bargained for.

ART FOR HEART'S SAKE

Perhaps your taste lies in another direction. The Courtauld Institute of Art, is a Mecca for those who enjoy art. They can be seen wandering round looking at the paintings and referring with an authoritative air to the catalogue in their hand. Such visitors often come in pairs, but the occasional 'single' might not be disinclined to have a chat about Matisse or other impressionists or a number in your catalogue, and who knows where the talk could go from there? However, I learn from someone who is more learned in the subtle art of seduction, that although walking round a gallery seems an ideal place for romance, there are certain hazards in this type of apparently neutral meeting place.

How do you keep in step with somebody, while at the same time showing your interest in them *and* the pictures on show? And what about the gallery itself? What pictures are they exhibiting? Some paintings, like some types of music, are more romantic than others. When the Hayward Gallery, for example, put on a 'singles' night, the work of Roy Lichtenstein was on display. However much you might admire the strong lines of this artist's work, and cool as he may be, he's not quite a lovebird's dream. Girls are hardly likely to experience heart throbs by looking at his work. Still, at £9 a night, the normal entrance fee, you could learn a lot by looking around, though the British Museum might be a better venue for more timid souls. If a rendezvous turns sour, you can vanish among the tomes.

FOOD FOR THOUGHT

Crowded restaurants, outside of busy lunchtimes, almost press intimacy upon you. So don't ignore such possible meeting places for the unattached as Patisserie Valerie in London's Old Compton Road and other alfresco dining areas where shared tables encourage talking.

Wandering round the corridors of the Albert Hall, or crushed into their crowded restaurant, you might find an opportunity for comment with the person pressed up against you, about the food, the crowd, what is to be seen or heard, and explaining how you managed to get such a good seat...

Alternatively try Sunday brunch and live jazz in concert at the café in London's Victoria and Albert Museum. If you take a book with an esoteric title, it is almost bound to catch somebody's attention. David Bowie used to carry a volume of Nietzsche in his pocket. He claims he never read it, but as a young teenager, found it attracted a 'better type of girl'.

Tate Britain/Modern similarly have a coterie of intellectuals, but of a quieter kind, unlike Irish bars which are full of blarney and where nobody thinks it unusual to talk with strangers. Irish bars in the UK may not be quite the same as the native kind, so cautions here are: don't drink too much, nor allow yourself to be escorted home by anybody who asks.

By contrast, you're unlikely to get the chance of drinking too much at winetasting weekends in the UK countryside nor, until the show is over, of going home with anybody. By that time you should have learnt enough to know the guests and grapes worth cultivating.

To combine whisky (or something less potent) with real Irish wit, take a Jameson Literary Pub Crawl from Duke Street, Dublin. You can see and hear professional actors performing the works of Ireland's great writers while you sip (?) your drink. (Contact Dublin Tourism or the Dublin Literary Pub Crawl on (0)3531 6705602.)

The National Gallery of Ireland boasts an interesting café in which you can buy several types of coffee including one which, the menu proclaimed when I visited the café, is made weaker by the addition of water. After 10am on Saturdays you will be back-packed up against tourists from all over the world.

If you are looking for a more moving experience, travelling to France by Eurostar gives you the opportunity for three hours' possible chat, enough for a lifetime and perhaps if you're lucky – a lifetime's partner, though it does seem to be going to extreme lengths in the search for Mr./Ms. Right. If you find him or her, however, you won't think the ticket price too dear, with Paris (and who knows what else?) at the end of the journey.

Local libraries list meetings and events taking place in the near future in their neighbourhoods. Join a Friends' organisation (not the Quakers but a society, theatre or place). You'll come across a wider sea in which to trawl your net. Details will be sent to you about the Friends' future activities: concerts, festivals, literary events, plays, tours. Some of the recitals offered by the 'Friends' of this or that town or organisation are by students hoping to make a career in the world of music. The performances do not cost very much and are of an extremely high standard, and there is usually some food and wine provided. Wander round, glass in hand, sizing up the 'opposition' before you go into the auditorium.

An extra advantage is that seats are not usually numbered so, unlike in a theatre, you can choose where you sit. Giving contributions to a particular charity, too, will mean you occasionally get invited (at a price) to some prestigious function where you will come across all sorts of interesting people from uncrowned heads to shooting starlets. The bonus is that part at least of the cost of your ticket goes to the charity you chose.

FOOD OF LOVE

Sometimes musicians, singers and players team up with other organisations like the Wine Education Service to provide snatches of opera accompanied by wine tastings. Hatstand Opera (Kirsty Young, director, www.hatstandopera.co.uk and enquiries@hatstandopera.co.uk) draws from a wide and varied repertoire of opera, operetta, song and classic musicals. The company have been touring for over ten years to audiences in village halls, castles, National Trust properties, art galleries and theatres. They have sung in Guernsey, in the open air, for conference dinners, Christmas concerts and charity galas from Aberystwyth to Wick, and in a vineyard in Western Australia on the same bill as Julio Iglesias.

At musical evenings in various central London venues organised by such organisations, songs are often coupled with tales of relevant paintings (in galleries) or with wine tasting and a buffet or canapés. You are welcomed into the foyer with a sparkling wine, then proceed into a dining room for a sample of wines which the cognoscenti can team up with the songs: *Die Fledermaus*, for example, with an Australian Semillon; Mozart's *Norma* with a Beaujolais, and a Bordeaux from the Haut Medoc with Puccini's *La Ronde*. If, like me, you find the connection so tenuous it escapes you altogether, or you don't recognise the music anyway, that will not spoil your enjoyment. There are always people around who know everything. By enlightening you, they enhance the pleasure of their evening ... and of yours.

FUN IN THE SUN

Holidays increase dramatically your chances of meeting different people. Unfortunately few tour operators appear to bother overmuch about singles, who always seem to get the worst rooms at an inflated price. Extra charges are the norm and no matter how brightly the sun shines outside, loneliness not empathy permeates your room like a damp fog. You might also find yourself in a group where the women think the men are going on 90 in outlook and perhaps in age, and the men regard the women as aggressive and defensive (against what?, one wonders). Far worse, however, is when the heady atmosphere of southern climes impels holidaymakers into risky situations. Get your E111 card before you leave the UK's friendly shores, and insurance for extra risks, or for special countries like the USA.

Example: Holiday risk

Mrs. Janette Pink, 44, ex-wife of a City accountant, claimed she was infected with AIDS by her Greek Cypriot lover, 39-year-old fisherman Paul Georgiou, after a holiday she took in Cyprus. He failed to tell her his wife Martha was dying of the disease and refuted her claim. Her life expectancy was reduced to two to three years and she brought a successful case against him for knowingly passing on the virus. The Cypriot law under which Georgiou was prosecuted was originally used to prevent the spread of cholera and typhoid. It carries a two year jail sentence and £1,500 fine.

Activity, villa and weekend holidays usually offer a good chance of mixing with like-minded company. But sometimes, the effort of joining in a group, particularly if it consists largely of divorced people who have been unhappily married or partnered and can't forget it, is very hard work. You come home from the venue feeling you want to remain single forever or, less dramatically, take another holiday all by yourself.

Nevertheless, hundreds of Shirley Valentines save up all year to set off from Southend or Solihull for Corfu or the Costas, hoping for romance under the Mediterranean sun. Some are lucky and find it. Most get palmed off with less. The glamour of an exotic terrain plays havoc with common sense. Read some cautionary tales, such as the one above, before snogging with native warriors, charming waiters, rugged fishermen, coralling cowboys, busty barladies, etc. – or even the sober English, let alone the drunks.

MATCHMAKING ORGANISATIONS

When neutral territory proves an arid desert with not a date in sight, you will have to look out for more fertile ground, such as marriage brokers and intermediaries, dating agencies, luncheon or dining clubs and similar organisations where there is a fee, sometimes a hefty one, to join. It could be money well spent, or money down the drain. There is no government health warning attached to the details you receive. Few married couples used to mention that they met through a dating/mating organisation, but now that this way of meeting is getting so much more common, partners are more open about how and where they met, especially when they split up to go their separate ways.

Personal ads and dating agencies still seem to carry something of a stigma. Don't let that deter you, but don't have illusions either. You may pay out a lot of money and get nothing but disappointment ... or worse. Take as much care in choosing an agency or answering a personal ad as you would in buying a house. (See Chapter 7 for more information.)

21ST CENTURY ISOLATION

People today lead busy, fragmented lives, often in towns where they have no relations and few friends. Their jobs take them all over the country. If they earn enough, and their job is likely to last, they prefer to buy their own flat rather than share the rent of a house with other tenants, especially in big towns like London. This leads to a more solitary existence with less chance of meeting others.

Career-minded people spend a long time in training, often moving from their home town to a place miles away and inhabited, so it would appear, by nuns or hermits. They may have come from families that have split up or migrated. In such circumstances it can be difficult to start up a relationship with anybody. There are 600,000 more single men than women in the 20–29 years age group; over a million people of all ages now live alone compared to 370,000 in the 1970s. Some at least would like a sympathetic friend or partner.

This desire for friendship/sex/romance/marriage is a human need, stronger in some people than others. History abounds with examples of 'brokers' asked to provide wives for kings and thereby heirs for a dynasty. Their efforts often proved disastrous for themselves and the luckless women who were brought to the royal thrones. Most of today's matchmakers have learnt from those mistakes. Some do a useful service by introducing men and women who may have little other opportunity for social mingling. These and other ways of meeting people and the cautions to take are described in the next chapter.

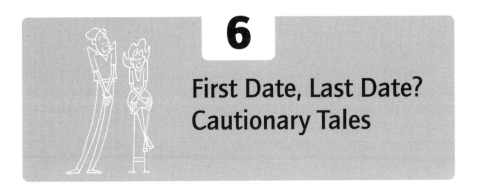

6

First Date, Last Date? Cautionary Tales

You've exhausted all the neutral territory with no luck. Acquaintances and relations have arranged parties for you with singles from hell. You send them back at your first meeting. What's next? The answer is territory designed for meeting people, sometimes many, sometimes a selected person or two. The Internet, text messages and phone chat lines can be used for introductions but classified adverts in magazines and newspapers are still among the most popular and the cheapest, though not always the best way of finding friends, romance and/or marriage.

CLASSIFIED ADVERTS

There is nothing new about such adverts. They have been going for a century since *Matrimonial Herald* published a quarterly list of some 200 lonely hearts, categorised into bachelors, spinsters, widowers and widows. The adverts proved so popular that they were copied by other newspapers. Working class men tended to advertise themselves as simple but honest, while aristocrats hid their search for moneyed heiresses by emphasising their own princely charms.

In the hope that they will attract people of like minds, today's advertisers use magazines or newspapers which reflect their own interests. Executive Mike Presdee of the British Sociological Association says that the pressure of work has led to this social phenomenon where people try to meet others through personal ads rather than the slower rituals of courtship. Mark Mason, a psychologist at Nene College, Northampton, trawled through 2,200 personal ads in local papers nationwide as well as *The Guardian* and *The Times*, to find what people were looking for in these columns and how they advertised themselves.

PUBLIC RELATIONS: PERSONAL CHOICE

Giving his results to the British Psychological Society in Edinburgh, he said that the best way to win a partner through such adverts was to stick to stereotypes. Few advertisers departed from convention. 'Genuine' was the adjective most commonly used, followed by 'humorous', 'attractive', 'caring' and 'loving'. Only two adverts in a thousand contained adjectives like 'fat', 'unattractive', 'cynical' or 'eccentric'. Desired ages varied. Men wanted women five to ten years younger than themselves, while women wanted men their own age or slightly older. These qualifications are not rigid, however. A glance at the *Evening Standard* personal ad column, 'Meeting Point' and similar ones elsewhere shows that advertisers appear less bothered about age than other attributes, often giving a range of ten or more years either way for their desiderata.

Describing themselves as attractive and highlighting their physical attributes may be the way men are responding to the fact that today's women are able to be more selective than ever before. They also know such adverts elicit more replies, with adjectives like 'genuine', 'sincere', 'high earning', 'humorous', 'caring' and 'loving' getting the maximum response. One query such descriptions might raise in a woman's heart is why such a prince among men has not been grabbed already. Ignoring that question, a suitable ad for a man to make might be as follows:

> *Male, 27, high wage earner, sincere and genuine with a sense of humour, seeks attractive, caring young woman for genuine partnership.*

At a recent wedding I attended, the 45-year-old groom, who had been married twice before, acknowledged at the reception that he had won his bride through Teletext. To be noticed first in the adverts, he described all his charms with the letter A: attractive, adventurous, amicable, etc., ending with available. The latter at least proved to be temporarily untrue for when the new lady love arrived at the arranged trysting place (a local pub,) there was no sign of the adventurous suitor. He had found it closed and gone off elsewhere. This is not an unusual scenario for such advertisements, but in this case there was a happy ending, as the wedding proved.

Heterosexual females look for rich men, at least rich enough to have their own home and car. Some might prefer, though never state, that only men with a bank balance of over £1m need apply. In return they offer the 'attractiveness' which men want, as well as the stereotyped female qualities such as young, loving and warm, which men also desired. Adverts most likely to attract a response from a man might therefore be worded something like the following:

Female, attractive, slim, tall, loving and sensitive, seeks caring, high wage earning man with sense of humour, own home, for genuine relationship.

UNDERGROUND ROMANCE

A different kind of advertisement in *Time Out* magazine's classified ad column appeals to travellers whose eyes met across a London Underground train. It seems that all is not lost if your tube train gets held up. Even tunnels can provide a semblance of romance. The ads read something like this:

21st June on the Central Line, 8.15am, Dark haired man, brown eyes, getting off at Oxford Circus; please make contact again with blonde woman travelling westwards with two Americans.

Sometimes coffee is offered as an inducement to a meeting. The good things about adverts such as the one above are that the advertiser and prospective date have already seen each other so they know at least what the other person looks like – and the closed circuit television is useful if things go wrong. The bad thing is that they might go wrong. There is a chance of rejection, of course, and an inherent danger for a woman of meeting a stranger about whom she knows nothing.

Thiry-two-year-old Daisy Garnett used the Internet. Her advert got 400 replies. With great difficulty, she chose five. All were possibles, but none of them worked out. She concluded that she would rather give over to fate and 'deal with the consequences or lack of them'.

Book researcher Rochelle Morton seems to have been particularly successful when she satisfied her curiosity and researched a book by using personal ads. Describing herself as 'mid-30s, fun loving, a non-smoker who likes to eat out', she got a 'staggering' response. Apparently ignoring the effect on her figure, health or purse, she breakfasted, lunched and dined with more than 700 'lonely hearts'. Some 75% of the replies were from people genuinely wanting company; 50% were datable and around 35% married. When she advertised for men in uniform she was swamped with replies from firemen, policemen and even an AA man.

DOUBLE MEANINGS FOR SINGLES

Some phrases appeared to have double meanings, changing the kind of response she got. Thus 'fun loving' or 'not wanting commitment' were interpreted as an open invitation for sex. She never went on a second date or had an intimate relationship with any of the men because she had a boyfriend whom she 'loves dearly'. He supported her in negotiating a publishing deal using the results of her research.

Some agony aunts think Rochelle took 700 chances too many. Their warning is very necessary, for it is not only the honest and lonely who use personal ads. Far from it, as a glance at any newspaper column will show. Some advertisers may have more sinister intent. This is why cautions are often displayed at the head or foot of the pages of personal ads.

SAFETY FIRST

As an example, the *Evening Standard*'s 'Meeting Point' ('The place to find romance, relationships or new friends') features a paragraph: 'Start Safe. Stay Safe.' It suggests that when meeting people for the first time, take all precautions to ensure your safety. Arrange to meet in a public place and leave details of your meeting with a friend. Keep your address and phone number confidential until you are sure you wish to continue the relationship.

Some organisations with on-line messageboards (and chatrooms) by which people can communicate with each other take extra precautions. Because the BBC's messageboards are read by people of all ages, including children, the BBC has set up a system of invisible 'moderators'. These invisible 'censors' read messages posted to the messageboards and remove those that break the house rules. In this case, a copy of the 'rejected' message is returned to the sender with the reason for its rejection.

In all meetings with strangers, it is better to be safe than sorry, as the following cautionary tales show.

Cautionary Tale 1

This message appeared in a lonely hearts column:

Company of female wanted with good sense of humour and TLC. Age and looks unimportant. I am 5ft. 8in, late 50s and well built. I would like a friendly relationship with no ties. I do drive. Please reply. Give me a try! Box number....

As a result of this personal ad, 63-year-old former taxi driver Brian Wolsgrove met more than 20 middle aged women in 14 months. He was reported to have had sex with some of them and ended up raping one, a widow. Convicted at Winchester Crown Court, he was jailed for five years. The victim's daughter had picked out the advert because he seemed 'genuine'. Her mother said he 'seemed such a gentleman'. She was so taken in by his charms that she invited him to her house, where the rape took place. Lonely people are often vulnerable. This is particularly true after the death of a loved husband or wife. Adverts in newspapers or on the Internet are not only from seekers of friendship. They may be penned by prostitutes. They may come from rapists, confidence tricksters or others of evil intent. Answering them means taking risks.

Cautionary Tale 2

Dr. Ann Mead was one of today's modern breed of women. Her demanding career as a GP meant long years of training. Her work brought her into contact with many people but she could not, as a doctor, be personally involved with any of them. In her mid thirties, wanting to marry and have children, she placed a lonely hearts advertisement in a magazine whose readers she hoped had interests similar to her own. Her search led to her murder by the lover she found.

STAYING SAFE

The following rules should help women avoid some of the hazards inherent in personal ads.

1. When you get a call from a man, don't go out with him if he sounds angry or weird or you don't like the sound of his voice.
2. Ring up the phone number he has given you to check that it's his, and hang up when there is an answer.

3. Never reveal your home address. Meet in a public place like a restaurant, pub or shop. Tell a friend/colleague/relation where you are going. In case anything goes wrong, give the phone number of your 'date' and where you can be contacted.
4. Devise some 'escape' routine, for example, a code word which can be given to a friend who rings your mobile at the prearranged venue and which can be used either to inform them that everything is OK or as an excuse to leave.
5. Don't accept a lift in the man's car. Use your own or order a taxi.
6. After three or four dates, you should have some idea of whether the man is 'genuine' or not. After that, you can decide what risks you want to take. Don't let sex be one of them, unless that was your intention in the first place and he knows it.

THE DANGERS FOR OLDER MEN

Because single men over 45 years in the UK are less numerous than women of that age group, they are similarly vulnerable to predators, but of a different kind. Their lives, too, may have been taken up with career moves with little time for personal relationships or commitment. They now find it difficult to meet the right woman: one without an existing family or not carrying some emotional baggage. Men like this, still youngish (when is a 'free' man ever old?), uncommitted and in short supply, are chased by status-seekers and gold-diggers or sought by broken hearts wanting a strong shoulder to weep on. Unlike women who can go on weekends or longer holidays with a female friend without causing any comment, eyebrows could be raised ever so slightly when two men travel together. How do they find the right woman?

Orthodox Jews consider finding a lifetime's partner too serious a matter to be left to the vagaries of fate. For decades they have used the services of professional matchmakers to ensure that marriages take place within and not outside their faith. The Jewish marriage broker is and always has been a much respected figure in the community. His job is to help people of the same religion meet and marry, not always easy when the community itself may be small or widely dispersed.

Example 1: Matchmakers – the marriage broker

Alex Stromm has been a matchmaker for the past 15 years. He charges £1,000 or more for a successful *shidduch* or match, usually paid for by the parents. Sometimes he merely gives a phone number to a young couple, but in more formal situations, the boy is approached rather than the girl, as it is important she should never be seen as being turned down. If the boy agrees, a meeting of the couple is arranged, usually in the girl's home. The pair are left alone for an hour or two to talk, and then give their reactions to the marriage broker. If it is favourable, they carry on meeting but with very rigid restraints. After the third date, Alex withdraws from the scene, and a marriage usually takes place within four to six months after the first meeting.

Love comes out of shared commitment, he declares, though there has to be some chemistry between the pair. It is their mutual goals that develop love.

Example 2: Matchmakers – the Jewish 'momma'

'Pesistence pays', said the brilliant lecturer at an investment seminar I once attended. He gave this example. At the end of a lecture in New York, a Jewish lady came up to him and said, 'Would you like to see a picture of your wife?' Intrigued because he was single, the lecturer agreed. The woman withdrew from her bag a picture of a really beautiful girl. The lecturer thanked her, returned the photo and managed to slip away. At his next seminar, the woman appeared again. 'I've brought your wife along,' she said, introducing the beautiful girl whose photo she had shown him earlier.

'That's not the end of the story,' he said and showed us a slide of the girl. She was stunningly beautiful. 'And here,' he continued, 'is my family.' Up came another slide... showing the same girl, now his wife, and their two children.

As there are fewer marriage brokers than formerly and for other reasons too, the editor of the *Jewish Chronicle* started an introductions column in the paper. It has proved an outstanding success. The editor comments that the pages are today's *shadchans* or marriage brokers.

The divorce rate among Orthodox Jews is certainly lower at 5% than among the population as a whole, but this may be due to the fact that divorced men and women are viewed with a certain amount of disfavour in their community. It is not only Orthodox Jews who believe in planned marriages. Many people in developing countries use the services of others to find marriage partners. And in the West, among immigrant but streetwise youngsters, the services of go-betweens are not unknown.

Example 3: Matchmakers – 'planned marriage'

Welcoming heads of state and other dignitaries to a conference in Maseru, the capital of his country, King Letsie III, the 33-year-old bachelor monarch of Lesotho, interrupted his prepared speech to explain a touching dilemma. 'The pressure on me to find a wife soon is heavy,' he said. Not only was he reminded of his dynastic duties by his mother but he found it difficult to meet other heads of state when they were accompanied by their spouses. Such sentiments might have been triggered off by the proximity of the young sixth wife of King Mawati of Swaziland or hearing about the wedding of President Mugabe of Zimbabwe to his young secretary Grace Marufu. The delegates, led by President Sir Ketumile Masure of Botswana, promised that each of them would provide at least one candidate for the young king. After news of his quest leaked out, local shopkeepers reported a run on fashionable dresses and make-up, while by some strange coincidence (?) a bevy of comely females was seen parading outside the palace.

Putting in your own adverts costs far less than becoming a member of an introductions agency, and you can choose which responses, if any, you will reply to. When you don't care for advertising your charms in the personal ads or scanning them to find other people as desirable as yourself, use different methods. Decide whether you want to meet a life partner or to widen your current circle of acquaintances. If the latter, go for some of the organisations mentioned in the previous chapter, or a semi-neutral situation like the once a week 'singles' nights run by some pubs, libraries, museums and supermarket chains with their special checkouts and music to serenade shoppers.

7

Making the Right Choice

CATCHERS IN THE WEB

If you're up to IT, you might try a bit of technology to find a soulmate. According to its development manager, more than 100,000 people have used the TV Teletext dating service and there have been at least 20 marriages and 10 children.

An even more popular form of personal ad are the websites which specialise in introductions and carry tens of thousands of 'dater profiles'. There are even cyber agony aunts, skilled in netiquette, who give advice to net Romeos and Juliets as to how to navigate through the sometimes treacherous surf. Online oddballs abound. Steer clear of them: cyber virgins are as vulnerable to online Casanovas as virtuous ladies were to more earthy swains in Austen's or Hardy's novels.

Some of the sites are devoted specifically to relationships. Others, like Compuserve's Connection Café, appeal to a wider audience. You can put personal ads in free of charge, chat about your love life or lack of it, and ramble on about your GSOH (good sense of humour) until you've bored your reader sick. This site generates about 1,000 messages a week, mostly by men. When you answer an ad, you type in your ID number but don't at this point have to reveal your name because it isn't added automatically to your reply which is sent anonymously across the Internet.

The ads are divided into regions covering Ireland and the whole of the UK with the emphasis on romance. General interest sections for pen pals, hobbies and lift sharing are also featured. The service is 'moderated' to eliminate rude or nasty messages, but cannot be 100% infallible, so be on your guard.

You don't have to be content with the UK. There are more fish in the sea than those that swim round our island waters; you can trawl the world with your net. If you have met some Lothario in France, Spain, Italy or the US, or a Nordic beauty/Moll Flanders on the way, they could prove initially more accessible via the Internet than meeting a real life Mr. D'Arcy or a lovely Lara in the UK.

It is well to remember that on-line introductions are in effect blind dates. You do not meet face to face, at least initially, so you learn about them not from their looks but only by what they say or any photos which they may send (genuine or not). You can portray yourself in any guise you like (the mind boggles). The fees are rarely displayed prominently and often extremely hard to discover even after perusing links and the frequently asked questions (FAQs) with the eagle eyes of a Sherlock Holmes.

Mark Griffiths, a psychologist researching technological addiction, says that on-line relationships can be very compelling, because people's inhibitions break down much sooner than if they met face to face. Meetings and marriages are possible after contact is made on the net, but difficulties arise when correspondents come from different parts of the globe.

To avoid disappointments or even danger, take precautions:

- Guard your anonymity and don't reveal your real name or phone number for several months or until you feel you can trust the other person.
- Don't meet a cyber friend in the 'real world' unless you want to. If you do, arrange the meeting in a public place during the day.
- Tell a reliable person where you are going, or take them along.
- Have a contingency plan ready in case things go wrong.
- Don't swallow, hook, line and sinker, everything you read or are told.
- If you get any pressure or harassment, report it to those maintaining the website.
- Don't get carried away by protestations of love. A lack of commitment or even dubious intent is often revealed by such words as 'should', 'would', 'if', 'perhaps', 'maybe'.

- Computers can be an addiction. Keep a sense of proportion and tear yourself away from the screen occasionally.
- Be patient. To establish trust needs time.

One caution, often ignored, is that international phone calls can make a big hole in your pocket.

Example: Expensive chats

When Robin Turner explored the Internet on his new computer he fell for Paula Rossi, a Brazilian girl, but even his six hour on-line sessions weren't long enough. He began making phone calls, and ran up a £16,000 bill in eight months. By that time, he had decided to marry Paula and leave his girlfriend of five years. Paula came to the UK, is now married to Robin and they are working out how to pay off the phone bill.

DATING AGENCIES

If personal ads in newspapers, magazines or on the Internet are not for you, take a look at 'luncheon' or similar clubs where people get together to meet others. Dating agencies have the same aim but on a more formalised footing. For a more permanent partnership, a marriage bureau is likely to be your best bet. Adverts on the Internet are censored to a degree by those who maintain the websites, (otherwise Heaven and Hell only know what might turn up – and occasionally does), but though there are trade associations, dating and similar agencies are not legally regulated. If they go under, customers may lose large sums, as happened in 1994 when three big agencies collapsed with debts totalling £1m. They left in limbo some 2,000 customers who had paid over £1,000 as joining fees. In the dating game, as in every other walk of life, cowboys operate. Make sure they don't take you for a ride.

Cautionary tale

A man who had set up a Birmingham based dating agency and several other outfits drugged and raped a prospective female client. He was jailed for 10 years.

Such happenings are rare, but greater care should prevent them happening at all.

When contemplating whether to join a dating/introduction agency or marriage bureau use the same principle as when buying a house (which might also have to last a lifetime), namely, *caveat emptor* or buyer beware. The organisation you choose will depend on your point of view, and depth of your wallet.

MARRIAGE BUREAUX

Marriage bureaux differ from other agencies in that their primary aim is to help clients find marriage partners. In this regard, they are unlike introduction services which simply introduce people seeking friends or temporary relationships. The Office of Fair Trading (OFT) suggests that before any fees are paid or any binding commitment entered into, a prospective client of a marriage bureau should be given a clear and simple written description of the service offered and the fees charged.

According to OFT guidelines, bureaux should:

- state whether or not membership is restricted to those currently unmarried. If, restricted,
- ask applicants to provide a signed statement that they are legally free to marry
- tell clients of the criteria used for matching and whether stated preferences are strictly kept or treated only as general indicators
- upon request give an indication of the likely number of introductions the bureau may be able to offer during the membership period, allowing for the particular circumstances and stated preferences of the client
- clearly state the fees to be charged, including any additional charges for interviews, further introductions, etc. or marriage
- offer clients the choice of a proportional refund or an extension of membership if the level of service initially indicated cannot be given.

INTRODUCTION AGENCIES

Some agencies charge dearly for a few introductions, none of which may prove suitable. At the outset ask for a printed list of the fees. Do not sign any contract which is not clear to you. Ask also whether all clients are interviewed or the agency relies largely on the filling in of forms. How many introductions will you get and what exactly is meant by an introduction? Will you be able to contact somebody in authority after you have joined? These are some questions you need to ask before signing up.

Check whether the agency belongs to a professional association such as the Association of British Introduction Agencies (enquiries @abia.org.uk, telephone 0845 345 2242). Ask for a list of their members. Lax security checks may mean lonely hearts dating with danger. Just as adverts attract the good and bad, so do agencies. Not all of them have experienced, honest managers. Caution is needed by people wanting to make genuine contacts.

Penrose Halson, who with her husband Bill ran the Katharine Allen Marriage Agency in London for 14 years, says, 'The whole area is a minefield'. Realising that many people were confused by the number and variety of introduction agencies, she and her husband created an on-line guide in whichintro.com. Mike Halson, Bill's son, is the director of a sister site, singleliving.com and another for travel companions. Fees are £20 for one year to whichintro, £72 for singleliving and £20 for travel companions or £65 for combined membership.

Mrs. Halson has a unique qualification in that she herself was a former client of the original Katharine Allen bureau when she was 27 years old but let her membership lapse until after she was 40. It was not a marriage bureau but a small ad for a lodger, however, that brought about her own marriage when she was 48 years old. 'Late developer,' she laughs. But she is very serious about marriage. She thinks commitment helps ride out the 'bumps' of living together 'and that the structure of marriage is the only practical way of organising ourselves as a society'. She quotes the fact that stress, illness and mortality rates are higher among divorced people and those co-habiting.

Dateline

This agency is reputed to be one of the oldest introductions agencies in Britain. Launched with 100 clients and a £1 membership fee, the escalation in numbers is reflected in today's price of £99 plus a monthly fee of £15. A week's trial membership is available. Dateline (www. datelinegold.co.uk) is not a marriage bureau but over 94% of the clients apparently join with a view to marriage or a long-term relationship, rather than to widen their circle of friends.

Sirius

Sirius (www.siriussynergy.co.uk), is unusual in having a voice message system. Users are given a number where they can leave a message for their prospective date. The organisation has branches in various parts of the UK and charges £495 plus VAT for one year's membership and £15 a month.

The forms which prospective members fill in are wide ranging. They cover education and qualifications and list items such as evening entertainment, general interests, musical tastes, sporting activities and personal qualities. There is also a column giving the member's religion, occupation and those of their parents, physical details and any known medical problems. If the depth of an investigative form alone could supply the perfect partner, this looks like a winner – but all is fair in love and war, and nobody who has paid nearly £500 in the hope of meeting a partner is going to describe themselves on a form except in the most highly desirable terms. However, they are interviewed during the form filling, so a man can hardly describe himself as six foot two when he is obviously a shade over five foot; nor a woman as slim when her girth fits into a chair.

Match.com

Match.com has 1.2 million registered users in the UK and 9 million in Europe. It is free to join and post details about yourself, your hobbies, interests, and the *desiderata* you seek. Personal details are kept confidential and when you send an email, are taken out of the message. Payment begins when you want to start contacting people. Membership costs about £17 a month with discounts available for three or six month packages. Match.com calculates that more than 200,000 members met the person they were seeking on the site in 2003 and outside. North America receives news of more than 100 marriages or engagements each month. Crunch question – how long did they stay with them?

Drawing Down the Moon

This agency caters mainly for professional people, of whom there are around 1,400 on its books. It started in 1984 in a bookshop near the British Museum and has since moved to Kensington, where staff can be phoned from 10am to 11pm seven days a week (www.drawing downthemoon.co.uk). Dinner dates (www.onlylunch.com), as well as the free site (www.loveandfriends.com) are part of the same organisation, run by Mary Balfour, reckoned by some to be the UK's number one matchmaking guru.

Classical Partners

An interesting and unusual agency 'restricted to unattached men and women... interested in music and the arts' is Classical Partners (www.classicalpartners.com.uk). Combining the functions of a dating agency, friendship circle and music club, it boasts some 1,400 clients, claims an average of six marriages a year and a 40% chance for clients of finding a soulmate. The fees vary according to the options taken, the most popular being the social membership (£495).

Members fill in a personal profile. The central section of this questionnaire, about yourself and preferred partner, analyses your musical taste by giving a selection of 30 composers and genres. Against these you tick 'keen', 'very keen' or 'enthusiast', according to your preferences. Photographs are affixed to the forms which are then sent out to prospective partners. First meetings take place at a music/arts venue. Sometimes this is a large event, sometimes in a less formal setting to promote young musicians. Taking place in private homes and with light refreshments, gives people an opportunity to mix and compare notes on the musical performance (and each other).

Dinner Dates

Dinner Dates (www.hillie.com) introduces people over dinner. Left with two small children after 18 years of marriage, Hillie Marshall divorced her husband in 1989 and started what is now one of the longest established and most respected dining and social events clubs for unattached single people in the UK. In the early days of Dinner Dates, Hillie hosted every event personally. Her natural warmth caused many members to seek her advice about a wide range of personal problems and she eventually became a listening ear for thousands. Dinner Date now boasts 14,000 members.

Hillie sees her organisation in the light of a social club more than a dating agency. There is a joining fee of £170 plus a standing order mandate of £15 a year. The average cost of a Dinner Date evening in London (less in other regions) is around £69, which includes pre-dinner drinks and a three course meal with wine and coffee at exclusive venues like Mosimann's, the Lanesborough, the Langham Hilton, the Kensington Roof Gardens and the Dorchester Club, but check prices before you go.

The evening begins with a drinks reception. After being introduced, guests are then seated at (usually) tables of eight, with place cards. After the main course the men swap places to pre-assigned seats on another table so that everyone sits next to four people of the opposite sex and converses with as many people as possible over dinner.

The following day Hillie and her team phone each guest to ascertain how he or she enjoyed the evening and to ask if there is anyone they met that they would like to contact. If there is, and only if both parties are agreeable, telephone numbers are exchanged. Dinner Dates also arranges events such as buffets, weekend breaks, sports activities and holidays at home and abroad.

Special interest groups

People who want to meet members of the same religious, ethnic, moral or cultural background can, with luck, also find these on the net. **Natural Friends**, for example, advertises itself (www.natural-friends.com) as 'the perfect introduction agency for ethically-minded, environmentally-sensitive, country-loving, health-conscious, single non-smokers'.

Full membership (90 days) costs £25.00, with the option of subscribing to the mobile text message service as an optional extra at £6.00 for 50 text units.

Vegetarian Matchmakers, for non flesh eating mammals and their possible mates, was established 24 years ago to bring vegetarians and vegans together. It is not just a 'dating agency' but offers friendship, social events and opportunities for members to publicise their own businesses and to develop other services of interest to the whole vegetarian/vegan community. Six months' full membership costs £45.00 or £65 for a year (www.veggiematchmakers.com).

People of different faiths or cultural backgrounds usually find friends and possible partners in their own religious institutions including mosques, churches, synagogues and associated clubs. When these prove too limited, to find others of like minds try newspaper columns or website introduction agencies. Muslimmatch.com, for example, is 'a matrimonial service which aims to unite Muslims through Marriage and Friendship' and by 'Using the latest in Internet technologies to promote love/compassion an understanding within the Muslim Community.'

Another option for those who perhaps want to meet only those of their own faith and culture is attending one of the special Christian, Jewish, Asian or Muslim 'speed dating' events.

The County Register is unusual in several ways. Firstly www.the countyregister.com accepts men and women from age 30 with the preferred age being over 45. Secondly clients are interviewed in their own homes, thus giving a good idea of their personality, standards and style before they get on the register. Once they are accepted, a fee of £8,000 plus VAT gives them 18 months' membership with six advertisements placed in quality broadsheets. The replies are screened and those deemed suitable are interviewed. The agency provides a detailed report on each of them and clients can then decide whether to go ahead.

One of the problems of the rich, apparently, is that they never know whether those who profess an interest in them are actually more concerned with their monetary rather than their personal worth. Founder Heather Heber Percy and her daughter Tamara guard the anonymity of subscribers and take the risk and embarrassment out of introductions. Travelling widely including visits to tax havens in search of the Right Person, they give no guarantee as to the outcome of their work except to say that subscribers will meet some interesting people.

At £8,000 a throw, this might seem a little on the steep side to those of us unacquainted with the problems of the seriously rich. The 'subsidiary' site, Portfolio Connection, comes in at only £1,500 for 15 months' membership and each fortnight sends out photos and descriptions of other members who can be contacted by subscribers.

Agency fees

Whichever agency you choose, think carefully about the cost in relation to what you hope to get for it, which may be disappointment and little else. For every success there are many failures and few people care to reveal that they met the love of their life through a dating agency. Tales abound of those who have joined agencies, often paying several hundred pounds to do so, without meeting anybody who remotely resembled a soulmate. Here are some of them, names and details suitably altered.

Example 1: Agency failure

Frank paid £400 for a year's membership of a London based computer agency and asked for someone aged between 35 and 55 with one definite requirement: he was passionate about showjumping and was looking for a woman who could share that interest. He got introductions to three ladies who hardly knew the back of a horse from the front. Meeting them for drinks, he says, produced the most embarrassing moments of his life.

Example 2: Agency failure

Kate, a 40-year-old widow from Scotland, paid a membership fee of £376 to an agency, and asked for a local non-smoker who could drive. She alleges that she was sent a string of unsuitable men, all non-driving smokers who lived 200 miles away, and is suing the company for the return of her fee.

Example 3: Agency failure

Mary, a single 40-year-old trainee physiotherapist, joined the London branch of an American agency. Interviewed in their office with high pressure sales technique, she paid the £1,000 membership fee on the promise of a personal service, and asked for a well educated, well read and sporty gentleman who lived, as she did, south of the Thames. He had also to be an animal lover because Mary kept a cat. The first man, an engineer, was nice enough, but lived in north London and would not collect her from her home because he didn't like cats. Number 2 was short, allergic to cats and definitely not sporty. Number 3 sounded nice but had put his membership on hold. She became more and more dissatisfied with the service, and finally wrote complaining about it not only to the agency but to its president in the US. He neither answered her letters nor returned her calls. She eventually got her solicitor to threaten legal action and went to Westminster

Trading Standards office. After appearing the next day in a TV programme she got her money back. The company closed down its UK operations in 1995 and Mary has given up agencies now. She would rather stay at home with her cat.

Example 4: Agency failure

In spite of her job as a journalist, 37-year-old Penelope felt lonely, but like most people in her position did not fancy joining a dating agency ... until her male flatmate told her he had done so and said, apart from the large cheque you had to hand over, becoming a member was painless. So Penelope filled in a detailed form about her likes, hobbies and preferred age range. Being 5′ 10″ tall, she also said the sort of man she fancied was one she 'could look up to'. Her first date was 'practically a midget', barely five feet tall. Candidate number 2, though loaded, was even more boring than he was tall (well over six feet). Nothing was really wrong with either of them but Penelope felt she had paid for her specifications to be met. They weren't. The next one was the wrong age. One dreary date followed another. She felt they, too, were being let down, having expected a voluptuous rather than the voluminous woman she was. She gave up when the last specification came through. None of her 'dates' had a single thing in common with her.

Agencies do, of course, have many satisfied customers, otherwise they could never continue in business. Here is the true story of one such success.

Example 1: Agency success

John became a member of a dating agency for one year in his early forties and again ten years later. (In both cases he was in a sought after age group.) Meeting more than a score of women, all genuine, sincere and lonely, he realised early on, as they did, that neither of them wanted to meet again. That first meeting, however, was a 'positive' experience of exchanging ideas and histories, and glimpsing how much care and humanity there was in the world. The woman he eventually married had already met three men through the same agency. She was beginning to give up, but agreed to meet just one more person. Then came the happy ending for both of them. Travelling hopefully may be worthwhile. Arriving is even better.

Difficult clients?

Sometimes it is the clients who are responsible for their own failures. They expect too much, the impossible dream. The owner of a provincial agency relates that a 49-year-old woman earning £12,000 a year would not be satisfied with anything less than a lord of the manor. Men, too, often have even more unrealistic expectations. Some come with a whole prospectus of the looks they require in a woman. Without their pockets lined like those of Michael Douglas, they hope for somebody resembling Catherine Zeta-Jones or a queue of Kate Winslet look-alikes lined up impatiently waiting for their call.

Another agency tells of a 50-year-old mother who joined with her daughter and got on with everybody, while the daughter found fault with them all. A man who mentioned church once was, in her eyes, a religious freak; another man with whom she had the briefest of meetings only ate Italian and that didn't appeal to her either.

A divorced man in his late fifties, whose wife left him for a younger lover complains – perhaps with some truth – that if a woman is single she is obsessed by her career and if she is divorced her concerns seem only to be her ex-husband, adult children or pets. He wonders why older women who think men are, on the whole, liars and philanderers ever join an agency in the first place. Hope over experience, perhaps?

Complaints procedure

There is no guarantee that by joining an agency you will find the man or woman of your dreams. But you should at least expect good service for the often considerable fee that you pay.

The Association of British Introduction Agencies (AIBA) can get agencies to look into your grievances or refer you to a low cost arbitration scheme; and if an ABIA agency goes bankrupt, its clients are taken over by another agency at no extra cost. Trading Standards offices and Citizens Advice Bureaux are also good ports of call for unsatisfied lonely hearts and often succeed in getting refunds for them. Sometimes a solicitor's letter will do the trick. But the strongest weapon of attack, when you feel you have not got the service for which you paid, is publicity. Of course, you might feel too embarrassed to go public, but it works.

SPEED DATING

This is an easy way of meeting a fairly large number of people, face to face, in a very short time. You contact an organisation such as SpeedDater (www.speeddater.co.uk 0870 300 3535) which runs singles events for 'professional people' in 'upmarket bars' throughout the UK and get a list of events. Having chosen a suitable one, you buy a ticket, which usually costs around £20 (dearer in large cities like London). At the event you are given a score card, pen and name badge and then have up to 30 three-minute 'dates'. The women usually sit at a table and the men move on every three minutes. You mark on the scorecard whether or not you would like to see any of your prospective dates again. You then log on to the website the next morning and enter your ticks online. Your results are immediately displayed, giving the names and email addresses of any 'matches' for follow up communication. So, if you have ticked eight people and find four of them have ticked you in return – bingo! – you have made four matches. Proceed from there.

SpeedDater is geared to Londoners, mostly under 35 years, though a new 35–50 group has just been set up. This site also advertises 'lock and key' parties, a variant of speed dating, costing about £10. On arrival, the girl is handed a padlock and has to find the man with the key to unlock it – not easy in a room full of perhaps more than 100 people. If successful both parties get a new key and lock and a raffle ticket.

To stray further, do a search for speed dating on the web – there is no shortage of sites and there are likely to be events in your local area.

HOLIDAYS

Perhaps you don't want to travel alone but would like a holiday. Travel Companions provides introductions for single people of all ages who want to go on holiday but not solo. Charging £15 (which might save the cost of the single person supplement) it is another part of the whichintro group (joining fee £20) which lists dating and introduction agencies (telephone 020 8762 9933).

ESCORTS

To conclude this chapter, mention is made of organisations which help unattached busy career women who might need a man's company when attending certain functions such as champagne receptions, society balls, private views at art galleries and similar events where it may seem better and more enjoyable to be a duo rather than a solo. In 2004, the cost of such escorts was £49 an hour for a minimum three hours, so you are paying nearly £150 for the privilege of a male arm. Sex is not on the agenda.

Cavendish Knights, based in Hampshire, is one such agency which supplies straight male escorts for a fee. They have over 600 escorts available in all parts of the UK but one day's notice is usually required for their services (www.cavendishknights.co.uk). No idea of matchmaking is involved.

Men like this job. It is well paid and much sought after because the women are not wanting anything more than an evening's entertainment. Their fee for helping her enjoy an event is very welcome; any expenses such as food and drink are paid for by her, and quite often the evenings help men adjust to having lost a partner of their own. A dinner jacket and tie with the right bearing are essential, otherwise if you are waiting outside a hotel (surely only a nerd would do so?) you might be mistaken for the doorman. Women find the service useful, particularly at night when they may not be too happy about travelling alone, although it is hardly likely to be used indefinitely except by women with the reputed wealth of Ivana Trump (and would they ever need it?)

Part Two

KEEPERS

8

Winnning Moves: Improving Communication

The crunch has come. You are meeting a man or woman for the first time. This meeting is no accident. It has arisen through an actual effort on your part or that of an intermediary, perhaps a paid one, because you are seeking a friend or a partner, perhaps a lifetime's one. You have memorised a few interesting or humorous anecdotes (and hope you can remember them). They might be useful to fill in gaps in the sparkling conversation you hope to achieve. You are looking your best and dressed appropriately for the occasion. Now, how do you start the ball rolling without scoring an own goal?

There are two options. The first is fairly easy. If you don't like the look of the person you find yourself with, and can't see yourself warming to them however long you stay or hard you try, don't roll the ball at all. Get away as fast as politeness permits. The fact that you cannot create the chemistry to fire up the senses is no reflection on either of you. You just haven't clicked.

The second option is when you like the look of your potential partner. How do you translate that first meeting into a second and third … and more? This is also fairly easy when you get a similar response, a helpful signal from the other side. But what if the only signals you get are negative ones? How do you manage then? You can give up. Accept that it's a no win situation and leave the venue, unrequited. Alternatively, you can try to make such an impression on the person that they remain staring into your eyes, wanting more … much more. (A likely story.)

ARE THEY REALLY SINGLE?

Before you go any further, make sure that the person you are meeting is single, not married or 'separated'. This check is normally done by the agency that sets up a meeting, but there is no harm in making sure as far as you can that, to use computer terminology, 'what you see is what you get'. This is not easy: no new acquaintance keeping a date will ever tell you that they are married – except as a prelude to a sob story about their imminent divorce. Teens and early twenties are unlikely to have ties. (Hire a private detective later, if you must.) A little subtlety is needed for older would-be sweethearts. Few people will take exception to a question about where they live. From here you can go on to ask about their house or flat and make sympathetic noises about costs. That should provide clues to the number of people living in your date's abode. But if you're worried, trust your instincts. Back off. He or she is not for you. Do not be inveigled into any relationship, however sweetly worded, if a current wife or husband is around, particularly if they have young children. Even if you are told that the marriage/partnership is dead, has been finished a long time ago, etc., you will be acting as the gravedigger or undertaker for the funeral. And if a husband or wife is ready to be 'stolen', statistics suggest that somebody else will play the same game with them later on. Keep your conscience clear.

FIRST IMPRESSIONS

Greet your date with a smile. Conversations, like a baby, are at their most vulnerable in the first few moments of life. If you happen to be very short, very fat or think you are otherwise not particularly physically well favoured, go ahead with your conversation, ignoring your apparent 'defects'. Being short has proved no obstacle to fame, fortune and romantic relationships. Short Spencer Tracy's affair with tall Katharine Hepburn lasted 26 years. The other approach is to draw attention to and make light of any apparent imperfections: 'I'm such a fat cat…' with a smile, 'because of all the money I'm making' or 'I may look short, but I'm growing fast.'

Looking ahead

Ruth Joseph met her husband Bernie through his secretary, a friend of hers, who said she knew somebody who would be 'perfect' for Ruth, although he was a bit short at

5ft 4in. Ruth had gone through two broken engagements and wasn't keen to meet this perfect man, particularly as her first two fiancés had seemed so absolutely right... on paper. When she met the new man, she got a real shock. He was actually under 5ft (and she was wearing high heels). But, says Ruth, his personality overshadowed everything. And though they have 'nothing in common' and she went through the terrible crises of three miscarriages before she had their two children, they have been happily married for 16 years.

WHAT TO SAY

Respond encouragingly to any comment made by your date. Ask them whether they like the venue. Unless you can make a joke about it, don't use the cliché, 'Do you come here often?' You're likely to get a better response if you say instead, 'I've not been here before. Do you know anything about (the organisation, the place, the conductor, the orchestra, the food)?' Add a comment to any remark your opposite number makes, to show that you have heard and taken it on board. You want to create an impression, to communicate well, so remember everybody at heart is an egotist. They like hearing about themselves. Mention to a journalist, for example, that you've read their latest outpouring, or to an author that you have seen their latest book. They glow all over.

Compliments are a great ice breaker. Go easy with them, however, otherwise they will prove not an ice breaker but a gob stopper. If you must shower your date with compliments, make sure they fall like the gentle rain from heaven. It's very easy to go over the top. To be on the safe side, when you make a personal comment or compliment that you fear might not be too well received, softly add the words, 'if I may say so.' If you receive a compliment, take it gracefully. 'Thank you' is never out of place. I once complimented an 80 year old on how fit and wonderful she looked. She laughed as she replied, 'But I am wonderful' – and who after that response could doubt it? After hearing about themselves, people like hearing about all the things that interest them. Never assume that other people, your dates in particular, are like you. It's the differences that often make conversation worthwhile. Be as honest as you can about yourself, but try and adapt to the other person's style. A quiet shy person might be attracted to someone who is extrovert and lively, but fear the lively one might be a bit too aggressive for comfort. A person who is more retiring may need to put a bit of effort into expressing themselves with more warmth.

Women like to express their thoughts, while men generally talk when they have something to say. So women appreciate a listening ear while men like encouragement for their contribution to a conversation; they want to feel needed. Ask questions that show you are interested in the person you are meeting, their pursuits or hobbies. You can get clues to these from the profile which an agency usually creates from their client's particulars.

HIDDEN LANGUAGE

You can also get clues to a person's feelings from their tone of voice or body language. The job is to interpret them. Words do not only convey meaning. They are a way of hiding them. Sometimes what people are feeling is obvious, sometimes not at all. They may speak hesitantly when they are embarrassed or unsure of themselves, a not unlikely reaction in the circumstances of a first meeting. But you could be very wrong in your interpretation, so don't rely on it overmuch. As an example, a frown can be a sign of concentration as well as of confusion or disapproval. British Telecom's *Talk Works* gives some clues to and questions on body language:

Body Language		**Feeling**
Arms folded	=	Defensive?
Shifting around	=	Pressured?
Tight lips	=	Angry?
Frown	=	Confused?
Holding breath	=	Tense?

ENCOURAGING CONVERSATION

Avoid questions that will only elicit a yes or no response. They are to conversation as a road block is to a moving car.

The following examples show the difference between the two types of questions.

For a yes or no answer	**For further discussion**
Have you seen (play, film, TV programe)?	What do you think of (play, film, TV programme)?

The following tips to open a conversation may help you get the attention of someone who appears, astonishingly, not to find you blindingly attractive:

Conversation openers

Dramatic: 'You'll never guess the amazing thing that happened to me on the way here' (or yesterday or last week). Say anything you can dream up that sounds exciting, convincing and however much exaggerated, is basically truthful.

Sympathetic: 'I'd very much like to hear what you think about...' Mention a current topic, an issue in politics, morals, business, etc. or comment on a case in the newspapers. 'What a very sad/horrific/terrible tale it was about ... Did you read it?' Don't be disappointed if the answer is no. You can then expand (not for too long) on the details of the sad/horrific/terrible tale.

Humorous: Recount any witticism, anecdote or aphorism that you have learnt from a book and adapt it to your present situation. (This may take a bit of homework.)

Controversial: 'I found what (a personage in the news) said/did today very brave/stimulating/disgraceful. How do you rate him/her?'

Youthful: 'What do you think of (latest single)?'

Good introductory lines are often heard at those *glitterati* affairs such as might have been presided over by Roy Strong in his heyday or currently at charity balls and rich people's birthdays. But you can go seriously wrong in trying out some of them. It's easy enough to pick out notables at such affairs, but how do you greet somebody whose face is familiar but whom you're sure you've never met before? If you say, 'Are you living in the same place?' as an opening gambit and they reply 'Yes, still at Buckingham Palace,' it can be a bit of a let down. And if you try to impress a colleague with your rich collection of notables by introducing one of them as 'The King of Denmark', and they say modestly, 'Sweden, actually', you could spend the whole evening living down your gaffe.

One of the best opening lines when you're meeting somebody in a crowd is the following, 'I can't recognise anybody here, but I suffer from prosopagnoia.' If you are then asked 'Whatever's that?' or a similar question, you reply, 'It's the failure of a person to recognise the face of any other person, however recently the aforementioned persons may have mingled in each other's company.' The definition is taken from Small's Enlarged English Dictionary, 13th edition (1806) and used by Colin Dexter as the prelude to Chapter 16 in one of his so enjoyable Morse novels, *Death is Now my Neighbour*. Like thousands of others, you have suffered from prosopagnoia in your time and experienced all the symptoms of this distressing complaint without ever realising it.

READING THE SIGNS

When dining with someone, remembering their name makes a good start to the meal. But whether you remember their name or not, you can tell whether you are holding their attention by tell tale signs. Are they fiddling with things in their hands, or, unless this leads to a comment about what they have seen, are their eyes looking round the room? Such apparent inattention may be because of boredom, in which case you have been as vibrant as a dead duck (change your tactics). Or it might be that your temporary partner has such difficulty in expressing their own thoughts and feelings to a stranger that their attention has wandered. They might be afraid of saying something that puts them in a foolish light or makes them appear vulnerable. Give them time and space.

The first attraction for men is usually physical, then emotional, followed by an appreciation of the other's spiritual worth. Women are usually first impressed mentally, then emotionally and physically, so **he** is likely to be more impressed with her body, **she** with his mind (and even his pocket). Being aware of these differences should make your first date easier and save you from a broken heart.

TAKE A CHANCE

Dare to be brave. Finish your appointment, lunch, dinner or musical evening and ask for another meeting. Nothing venture, nothing gain. Read Jane Austen's letter to her sister, Cassandra, to see how a young man lost the chance of Jane as a bride.

*There was one gentleman, an officer of the Cheshires, a very good look-
ing young man who I was told wanted very much to be introduced to
me, but as he did not want it quite enough to take much trouble in
effecting it, we never could bring it about.*

Don't follow the example of this faint-hearted good looking young man
of the Cheshires who, apart from this reference, has faded into obliv-
ion. You have a 50% chance of getting the right answer. And when you
don't get the response you want and go on the date of your dreams,
remind yourself that all is not lost. There are plenty more fish in the
sea. Keep your net by your side.

WHAT IS YOUR STYLE?

If you are lucky (?) enough to arrange another meeting, you might like to
think about improving your communication skills. One way could be by
what sounds a real turn off: neuro linguistic programming (NLP).
Practitioners of this therapy swear (in a manner of speaking) by it, and
say that its techniques can help you find true love, the ideal job, bolster
up your self confidence and improve your relationships. Extravagant
promises, but do they work? The best answer is probably to try them and
see. Sports people are supposed to have improved their performance,
film stars their auditions by its use, and Bill Clinton is rumoured to have
been helped to win the presidential election through NLP techniques.

Developed over two years in California (where else?) and now part of
some university courses in America, NLP is the study of what works in
thinking, language and behaviour. It also looks at ways people relate to
one another and how to improve that relationship through the 'sensual
wavelengths': visual, hearing, or touch-sensitive (kinesthetic).

When people are in love, these wavelengths do not matter. The desire to
please overcomes all barriers, although the couple will revert to their
'wavelength' types eventually. For others, knowing their wavelength and
the body language that goes with it, helps, so it is said, to develop a relationship. You can ascertain from a few questions whether you are a
looker (visual), listener (hearing) or toucher (touch-sensitive). There is
no category of talker, though how you can find a listener without one is
not made clear. Here are a few clues as to which kind of wavelength
you have and which might help you on your first date (or your last).

Lookers

Lookers are impressionable. They make up their minds about people from their appearance, are impatient and impulsive but well organised and well groomed. They like eye contact and dislike being interrupted although they will quite happily interrupt others to establish a point. They enjoy going to new places and like to be complimented on their appearance.

Listeners

Listeners enjoy conversation and music. They listen intently to both and learn more easily by hearing than seeing. They often veer to jobs in accountancy because they can aurally digest facts and figures. Being told at work how well they are doing is essential to their progress and they also like being told by friends or spouses how much they are loved.

Touchers

Touchers are sensitive, tactile, sometimes moody. They enjoy being the focus of attention, like company and may get depressed without it. Experiencing life through their feelings sometimes makes them appear inattentive, and when talking they may move around or fiddle with objects in front of them. They respond to words which relate to them, and often stand close to people. Their handshake is warm and firm and they use their hands when they talk.

Compatibility

The following tips tell you how best to develop a relationship within those categories:

Visual man, visual woman

They love TV, cinema, receiving presents from each other and must avoid signs that indicate, wrongly, they are interested in somebody else.

Visual man, hearing woman

She prefers hearing sweet nothings to receiving flowers, he, visual language to prevent his thoughts slipping elsewhere.

Visual man, touching woman

He wants gestures from her but must restrain his jealousy if he sees her innocently touching others.

Visual woman, hearing man

They enjoy TV and theatre, but she needs evidence such as a surprise gift, when he says he loves her.

Hearing man, hearing woman

They must learn to talk to, not at, each other, otherwise in spite of their conversation, there will be no communication between them.

Hearing man, touching woman

She wants demonstrations of affection; he wants to hear them.

Visual woman, touching man

Both understand each other's body language but sometimes avoid talking about important issues. They need to compromise about their different interests.

Hearing woman, touching man

She wants to hear him say 'I love you', can help him talk about his deep feelings but must avoid overwhelming him with chat.

Touching man, touching woman

This usually works out well physically but tempers are often on a short fuse and feelings can be hurt.

For more information about NLP, check out www.anlp.org or phone the Association for Neuro Linguistic Programming on 0870 787 1978.

IRRESISTIBLE YOU

Also from America (where else?) is Irresistible Attraction, a course organised by Attraction University, the brainchild of Thomas J Leonard who set up Coach University in 1990, which enabled students to learn on the phone from home. He sold it in 1996, for $2 million. In the 12 weekly hour-long phone sessions, you first list all the things you are putting up with (the average is 60–100). This exercise releases your energy. Then you list your deepest emotional needs and work out a system to meet them, focusing on your strengths not weaknesses. That builds up confidence. You learn to be honest, not pretend to be what you are not, nor too concerned with the results of your daily life

You consider what you offer other people; give more than your best and are generous without thought of gain. You learn to treat everybody with respect and compassion.

A cheaper method than the American course might be to learn and obey the Ten Commandments, but the Irresistible Attraction course makes you, so we are told, irresistibly attractive whereas the Commandments promise no such thing. One poor fellow I knew, who began carrying out literally the precept of giving up everything to the poor, landed in a mental hospital. By contrast, Irresistible Attraction makes your life easier, more fun and (wait for it) more lucrative. After such an induction, you should end up if not the most attractive person on the block (in the office, etc.), certainly as a lookalike Mother Teresa, though somewhat richer. But, wait for it, the Attraction principle does not confine itself either to the material or the spiritual. You can have it all: integrity AND compassion AND success. Even a woman, physically unattractive (are there any?), dull and boring, can get energy and confidence through the course, the two most attractive qualities, so it is said, anybody can possess. If you are thinking of the course as a prelude to the wedding march, however, think again. There is an unfortunate let out: if a woman feels the need to get married too strongly, she loses her attraction. To become more attractive, she must become less needy because everybody is at their most attractive when they are content with their life the way it is.

9

To Wed or Not to Wed: Cohabitation Versus Marriage

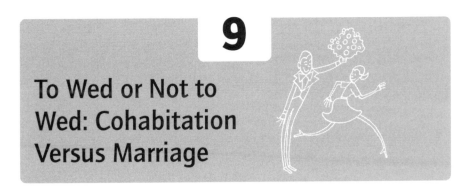

Until the beginning of the 20th century, it was assumed that an unmarried woman, unless she was a nun, had missed the chance of marriage. She got the epithet of 'old maid' when barely 30 (with quite different connotations from 'old bachelor'). Nobody thought she could ever refuse a proposal however unattractive the suitor, or that she would voluntarily choose to remain unmarried. The sole reason for her single state was because no man had asked her to be his wife. Pressures of this and other kinds often forced women into loveless marriages. Marriages were also the result of conquest, wars or treaties. Sometimes payment might be asked or offered for a bride. A bride price is rarely heard of today, but only 30 years ago, African students in London might joke about a female accountancy student, saying that her qualifications made her worth a bigger bride price, two cows perhaps instead of one.

Economic or social pressures did not unduly affect rich women. They had plenty of applicants for their hand and what went with it. Unless a dynasty, title or treaty was involved, or they were very young, they accepted or rejected offers as they pleased. For poorer women, it was different. Marriage provided for them and their children, financial security and status, in theory if not in fact.

MODERN RELATIONSHIPS

With the coming of the welfare state, and the liberalisation of laws on illegitimacy, abortion and divorce, such pressures disappeared. Religion, however, still has a strong influence on marriage partners.

Parents, too, for these or other reasons (financial, dynastic, tribal, social) are sometimes extremely forceful about whom their offspring should wed. These pressures linger on in certain countries, and within some immigrant families in the UK who bring their own customs with them.

Religious/family pressure

Wealthy restaurant owner Abdul Hoque and his wife Ayesha Khanam brought their family up as Muslims. It was likely if not inevitable that their daughter, 20-year-old Zinat, would have an arranged marriage. When she began a relationship with Roger Allard, a jobless West Indian, she knew her parents would not approve, secretly moved her belongings to his flat and left home. Her appalled father tried to end the relationship by buying off the 'suitor', asking him to name his price. When the offer was refused, he hired two men to kidnap his daughter. She was bundled into a car driven by her father to a hideaway and two days later to another address where she was held for seven days before being freed by police. Hoque and his wife were found guilty of false imprisonment and conspiracy to kidnap; a relative of conspiracy to kidnap; and the victim's brother, of false imprisonment.

However, the majority of western women today have choices never previously open to them: sex without marriage, sex without children, children without sex and children without men, or at least without a man's physical presence. 'Beddings', though still not as popular as weddings, have become more acceptable than ever before. The lifestyles of women in developed countries today, with independence, professional careers and incomes of their own, were never available to their mothers or grandmothers. Today's women no longer need men to support them financially and seem to want love not marriage, apparently assuming that one excludes the other.

The attitudes of 50 years ago: of marriage, sex, children, in that order, of choosing between sin for earthly pleasure, abstinence for heavenly joy, have disappeared. With them have also gone words suggesting impropriety or immorality. Euphemisms have taken their place, such as 'love child' for the cruel epithet of 'bastard', and 'gays' replacing the equally unkind 'queers'. 'Friends' can mean anything from a long-standing sexual relationship to the innocent liking of one person for another and 'partners' no longer refers only to business associates. Romance is still with us though no longer coupled with marriage, which is fast becoming a threatened institution.

Romance without marriage

In a romantic couples competition, Jeremy Green (23) and Kate Dicken (21) beat 120 other pairs to win the accolade Young Lovers of the Year. Kate said her boyfriend often surprised her with love notes and gifts, even a trip to Venice. They had no plans to marry as they feared it would destroy their relationship: 'when you are going out with someone, you make more of an effort'.

When a couple enter into a partnership or relationship, become an 'item' or whatever a temporary sexual pairing of a man and woman may be called, they can terminate it without legal difficulty. Ending a marriage costs legal fees and possibly months or years of acrimony, but the tie can always be ended by divorce after five years at most, even against the wishes of the other spouse. So, the argument goes, what's the point of marrying? Why not just slip into bed together, enjoy life and when the enjoyment passes, go off with somebody else?

This is not such a halcyon existence as it sounds. Enjoyment is not always easily come by, in spite of today's craving for happiness. Though around one marriage in four ends in divorce, unmarried partnerships break up even more frequently. So if a child arrives, wanted or not, it can be a spanner in the works.

Entente cordiale

One solution currently dreamed up in France is what might be called a little bit of marriage, through a *pacte civil de solidarité* – a sort of civil marriage with three months' notice either side, in other words a toe in the water and if it proves too cold, or a storm threatens, a hasty run back to the safety of the shore. Aimed at heterosexual and homosexual partners, the *pacte* has attracted 10,000 gay couples.

Britain is on the way to a similar register for gay couples with the London Partnership Register, the first registration, having been launched at the Greater London Authority's headquarters (£85 fee), and the Civil Partnership Bill became law in November 2004.

HAPPILY EVER AFTER?

Breakups of any kind are rarely happy affairs, and even a three-month *pacte* may have its tears. When a couple decide to live together, they usually assume *their* relationship will be a happy one. *They* won't split up. They don't want to marry, just to try out whether the set up will work. In most cases, the situation lasts, at best, for a few years. Some crisis, perhaps financial, domestic (relations), or the question or advent of children, later arises. It threatens the relationship and causes the pair to part. Married, they might try more strenuously to overcome the hurdle.

However, living together has grown increasingly popular, particularly amongst women with dependent children. In 2001, over 69% of cohabiting women aged 16 to 59 with children were unmarried. The number of women under 60 cohabiting has doubled from 13% in 1986, the first year data was available, to 28% in 2001/2. For men, too, it has more than doubled over the same period.

Example 1: Living together

Vicky and Paul are both 27. They have been living together for three years and prefer partnership to marriage, one reason being that they are both very high earners, with Vicky having an independent lifestyle that includes a lot of travel. She doesn't want to feel trapped into a marriage which may limit her freedom. The second reason is that Vicky and Paul come from 'broken' homes. Vicky's father left his wife when the children were small, while Paul's mother went through an acrimonious divorce. Vicky and Paul don't want to repeat this experience. Thirdly, Vicky loves horses and riding; Paul is mad about golf. As partners they can each enjoy their own sports without resentment of the time taken up by the other outside the home. In addition, Vicky would like children, but Paul is not interested at the moment, so they remain as partners for the time being.

As with cycles of deprivation, it often happens that children of divorced parents repeat the experience of their parents, or try to avoid it by opting out of marriage altogether. This is what Vicky and Paul have done.

There are several things to take into account when considering marriage or a looser tie. Marriage may appear more restricting than 'living together', but it provides a basis of emotional security, the understanding that your partner is less likely to disappear within the next few weeks into somebody else's bed. It is not only a commitment to each other but a declaration to society of that commitment, protecting a couple, to a limited degree, from sexual predators.

A wedding is also an opportunity for celebration and enjoyment by the nuptial couple, relatives and friends. This cannot, of course, be considered as a reason for getting married. It is merely the icing on the cake. But opportunities for family 'get togethers' other than funerals become fewer as families split up, migrate, age, lose touch or give up their religious festivals. Such celebrations need not be costly, as is often claimed, and act as a 'lift', a boost to what is for many people their prosaic daily routine.

Example 2: Living together

Mark is 41, Janette 38. Both are divorced with children. Mark's two boys live with his ex-wife and her new partner, while Janette's one son lives with them. Mark would like to marry Janette but she prefers to cohabit. Her divorce was such a shattering experience she feels she just cannot risk another marriage in case it ends in disaster.

The above true life stories show examples of people in different age groups who prefer an unmarried partnership to marriage. None of the pairs had religious or moral scruples which might have caused them to hesitate before making this choice. But neither appeared to have given any thought to the legal or financial aspects of their choice, either.

Living together: some figures

A survey by the University of Essex on life in Britain in the 1990s, based on interviews with 10,000 adults, showed that parents who cohabit are four times more likely to split up than those who are married. Half of unmarried couples who have children split up within ten years, compared with one in eight where the parents are married. According to the authors, permanent relationships of people who live together without marrying are rare. Pro-marriage groups emphasise that cohabiting is a very fragile situation, and it is the children who suffer.

WHAT MAKES A MARRIAGE?

Marriage is a contract with rights and obligations. In this light, it makes sense to consider what is the better option: to be a live-in-lover or a spouse. A valid marriage (and there is not much point in considering anything else) must be (a) voluntary (b) between two single people (c) over sixteen and (d) of the opposite sex (e) who are not related. The 'opposite sex' clause has been weakened somewhat by the gradual introduction of such unions as the French *pacte* or in some countries, 'gay' marriages, one reason for which is to offset the very unfair social security and tax situation during the lifetime of the partners or when one of them dies.

(a) Voluntary

Both parties to the marriage must be acting of their own free will, not under force, fear or duress. If either of them do not realise what they are doing because of drink, old age, insanity or other causes, the marriage is not valid.

Example: Non-voluntary marriage

Under the threat of being thrown out penniless from her parents' house, a Hindu girl of 19 was forced into an arranged marriage. The Court of Appeal judged that the pressure of homelessness and social ostracism was sufficient to destroy the validity of the marriage and it was annulled.

(b) Single people

In the UK, the two people coming together must be single, widowed or divorced. If polygamous marriages have been made in their own countries, English courts will normally recognise the marriages, if they complied with the law of the country where they took place.

(c) Over 16

Before 1929, the minimum age for marriage was 14 for boys and 12 for girls. It is now 16 for both. If a boy or girl marries under that age, the ceremony is null and void and a criminal offence is committed.

(d) Opposite sex

Marriages between lesbian and gay (homosexual) partners have in some countries a legal validity. Intending marriage partners should check their own laws or consult a solicitor. If such marriages are not valid there, they should make individual wills to ensure that their partner does not lose out financially upon their death. This is particularly important if they share a home.

A marriage where one of the partners has had a sex change can be invalidated.

Example: sex change

April Ashley, born a man, had a radical sex change operation in 1960. Three years later April met a man who knew about the sex change. They married and lived together as man and wife for three months, when the man asked for the marriage to be pronounced null and void as it was between two men. The Court judged that it was not a valid marriage because April Ashley had been born a man, and by all medical criteria, although psychologically transsexual, still was. The sex change had not altered his biological (legal) sex and so the marriage was void. Further, the marriage could be annulled on the grounds of non consummation because the artificial vagina did not admit full intercourse.

(e) Not closely related

Marriages between people closely related to one another are generally prohibited in England. This can include divorce or adoption. Thus a man can marry his cousin, but not his brother's adopted daughter or the divorced wife of his son (though why he should want to is nobody's business). In some countries, to continue an established family connection, marriages within the family are encouraged. The ancient Hebrews allowed a man to marry one or more of his wife's sisters, perhaps if the wife had died or could not have children. It was also permitted for a man to marry the widow of a deceased brother.

Had such a custom been permitted in 16th century England, Henry VIII would not have needed the papal dispensation which allowed him to marry Catharine of Aragon, his brother's widow. He did this a month after succeeding to the English throne. Catharine bore him six children of whom only one, Queen Mary I, survived. Some 18 years later Henry tried to annul the marriage, so that he could marry Anne Boleyn with the hope of a male heir. The Pope refused to make a decision on the annulment and Henry was married to Anne Boleyn by the Archbishop of Canterbury. A year later the Pope declared the first marriage to be valid. Henry thereby became alienated from the Catholic church and the way was opened for the Reformation and the Church of England with its own marriage rites.

THE 'COMMON LAW' WIFE

No matter how long a couple live together, English law neither recognises nor provides any protection for a 'common law' wife if the partnership ends. Not regarded as of much importance to most couples, it could become so as they get older or if they want to sell their house. In Scotland, the law is different: couples who have lived together for a long time are treated as if they were married ('marriage by custom and repute'). But the common law wife is at a financial and legal disadvantage in many (but not all) ways compared with a married woman.

As an example, unless she is the owner or joint owner of the house in which she and her partner live, she can only exceptionally claim a share in its value. If children arrive, always a possibility, she can claim maintenance for them, but not necessarily for herself. She is not entitled to any part of her cohabitee's state pension nor of an occupational one unless he makes a specific arrangement with the pension fund trustees. If he dies without making provision for her in his will, she can claim no part of his estate.

The position of the unmarried father is much worse. Although he has to provide maintenance for his children, mothers have sole parental responsibility. He has no rights at all, only duties, and may find it very difficult to get access even if it is provided by a court decision.

Some of the financial difficulties arising as a result of a breakup of an unregistered 'partnership' are today offset by social welfare benefits. These could change at any time and not necessarily for the better.

Children need fathers, particularly as they grow older, yet according to the latest available figures, Britain has more single parents than any other country in Europe. Nearly 150,000 children under 16, of whom 34,347 are under five, will see their parents split up. The subsequent scenario is not likely to improve family relationships and may lead to teenagers preferring the streets to their home – if they get a choice and are not kicked out first.

The following table shows some of the **current** differences between a married and unmarried couple (likely to alter if registration of couples of the same sex is introduced).

Some differences in the legal position of married and cohabiting couples

	Married	Unmarried
MAINTENANCE for **each other**	Each has a duty to maintain the other; sometimes, by court order after the marriage as well (see example below). If maintenance is paid out of the husband's net income the wife does not have to pay income tax on the amount received.	Neither has a duty to maintain the other at any time.
RIGHTS over the children	Husband and wife have an equal say in the child's upbringing. If it is in the child's interests, the courts can make an order for residence, contact, etc.	The mother has sole parental responsibility. The father can acquire this by agreement with the mother or by court order. Only in an exceptional case will the court grant him a residence order.
'family' home	(a) Both have equal occupation rights until marriage ends and (b) right to half share thereafter BUT note capital gains tax advantage for an unmarried couple if each has their own home.	(a) The owner only has occupation rights. A partner can be evicted after due notice unless an injunction excludes the owner because of violence or other causes (b) entitled to nothing when the partnership ends except what is legally hers or if she can show she has enhanced the value of the property.
TAXES (a) income	Each has own tax allowance but also a married couple's allowance which reduces the husband's tax bill unless his income is too low to take advantage of it.	Separate assessment; single person's allowances only.

(b) capital gains	A gift between spouses attracts no tax. If for example, a husband gives a gift worth £8,000 which cost him £1,000, to his wife, she is not liable for CGT (but could be if she later sells it.)	Any gift above the exemption allowance for that year, could give rise to an immediate chargeable gain.
	BUT NOTE: only one principal residence exemption allowed.	Each has a private residence exemption.
(c) capital transfer	Transfers between spouses, exempt.	May be taxable.
(d) inheritance	A spouse does not have to pay tax on the benefits from a deceased partner's will. Gifts made during the marriage are also exempt.	Tax payable if over the normal exemption allowance.
*BENEFITS		
(a) state pension	A wife may claim a pension on her husband's NI contributions as well as qualifying in her own right .	No entitlement to a state pension except by her own NI contributions.
(b) occupational pension	Widow usually has pension rights.	No pension rights for survivor, unless specifically applied for and agreed with the pension provider.
(c) widow's benefits	Allowance and pension.	None.
(d) maternity grant	On own NI contributions or husband's.	On own NI contributions only.
(e) maternity allowance	On own NI contributions.	On own NI contributions.
IMMIGRATION	Either can usually join spouse in UK.	Unlikely.

* Subject to alteration with new budgets and laws.
Note: Intuit's software *Quicken* XG 2000 offers a quick guide to financial issues such as tax, debt and retirement.

Example 1: Maintenance after marriage (old style)

In 1969 a £4,000 a year car dealer, who was being divorced by his wife for cruelty, said she had brought nothing into the seven year marriage except 12 packets of crisps and a trifle over £4. She disagreed, saying she had also provided a packet of Ritz biscuits and 1/2lb of margarine. Her husband said she could have a £75 lump sum, £12 a week for their two sons and a Mini. She moved out of the £4,000 home and into a £5 a week council flat, but within weeks, her ex-husband moved in with her and they stayed there, divorced and unmarried until 1973, when they moved into a £26,000 detached house in an exclusive Southampton suburb, where in 1974 their third son was born. Twenty years later when her husband's business was prospering with a turnover of £3m, he began an affair with her best friend and moved out.

The ruling by the High Court in 1996 that the ex-wife was not entitled to more than the original settlement was overturned by the Appeal Court. It ruled that if pre-marital cohabitation can be considered in divorce settlements, post-marital cohabitation should also count. Lord Justice Ward said that delay was not a reason for closing the door upon her, and that if the court did not intervene she would suffer undoubted hardship; the ex-husband had the means to redress it. Lord Justice Ward said that the county court judge to whom she must now apply for a new settlement would have to consider how much she had contributed to the welfare of her family.

Today's long delayed emphasis on equality assumes that both partners suffer equally after a marriage breakdown. This may be true emotionally, but not always financially. Only the rare high earners can maintain two families. If women are the higher earners in a marriage which breaks down, they will have to 'maintain' the husband.

Example 2: Maintenance after marriage (new style)

Famous novelist Fay Weldon relates her horror when in 1990 she discovered that, as the higher earning spouse, she would have to share all her worldly goods with her ex-husband, no matter what the reason for the breakup. The ideas of fault, innocent and guilty had disappeared.

ADVANTAGES FOR 'SINGLES'

As the table shows, a UK unmarried couple has two financial and legal advantages compared with a married pair. The first is the exemption on capital gains tax where each owns their own house. The unmarried will have to work out how they can live together in separate establishments. Some do. Either residence can be sold without gains tax applying, whereas a married couple have this tax exemption on one principal private residence only. The second advantage is more controversial: a marriage can only be ended by court order (divorce, nullity, etc.) and it costs. A DIY divorce is possible when there are no assets and nothing financial to quarrel over. Solicitors' fees do not come cheap. If there is disagreement between the parties over the financial 'spoils', legal costs could mount astronomically and the 'losing' side may have to pay all costs plus the legal fees of both parties. If you are merely cohabiting, of course, there is unlikely to be any need for lawyers should the relationship end.

Legal Aid

If you need legal help sorting out your previous marriage or relationship and cannot afford it, you may be able to get legal aid, from the Legal Services Commission. There are different systems in Scotland and Northern Ireland so contact a website such as the Legal Services Commission (www.legalservices.gov.uk) and read their guide to the Community Legal Service. Details of LSC approved solicitors in your area are at www.clsdirect.org.uk.

SOURCES OF LEGAL HELP

For sexual or emotional problems, newspaper and magazine 'agony aunts' provide helpful, down to earth and often amazingly simple solutions. Slightly quicker answers and much else come from www.relate.org.uk which 'helps parents and young people in their family life'. (For appointments, phone 0845 456 1310, Mondays to Fridays 9.00 to 5.00 'with credit card handy'.) Another source of information, guidance or assistance is the Citizens' Advice Bureau, also available online (www.adviceguide.org.uk). Though the bureaux tackle problems mainly concerned with housing, welfare benefits and social security, they can also suggest the names of local solicitors who offer a free or fixed-fee initial interview.

Grant-funded Law Centres provide free and independent legal advice and represent people in legal proceedings. Be clear about what you want from a session and go with any papers/documents relevant to your case. Other problem solvers are Age Concern and trade unions, which have a comprehensive guide to obtaining and paying for legal advice. You can also download from www.lawsociety.org.uk (phone 020 7316 5605) customer guides to using a solicitor, setting up home with your partner, getting a divorce and other financial or legal problems.

An unmarried partnership ends when either partner so chooses. Whether this is more advantageous than the tighter bond of marriage, only the partners or spouses themselves can decide. When there are children, there is no question: marriage nearly always has the edge. If love's young dream is to last – and why not? – the partners and any children from the relationship are better served by marriage. A good choice of partner helps to achieve this. Top earners, film stars and other celebs often sign prenuptial agreements ('With all my wealth I thee endow, except the bits and pieces I've kept as per the prenuptial agreement'). This may shorten rather than lengthen the marriage if either partner becomes strapped for cash, but may also serve to make a divorce less acrimonious.

A WORD FOR 'SINGLES'

Men generally need company and can usually find it. If a woman prefers to remain single, why not? Ignore predictions about a nation of singles. You want to live **your** life ... then again, why not? There are many advantages in being single: friendships; spontaneity; freedom to do what you like when you like; ability to pursue a career or profession to the top if you wish. There are also many advantages in being married: company, security, multifarious interests, shared chores (though this needs a bit of training and taming), laughter and love.

There are no advantages whatever in being single or married if that state, and that state alone, causes you to be unbearably unhappy. Change your role, whatever it is, but do not forget that how you feel in your twenties is going to be very different from the feelings you will have at 50 or 60. The aging process reveals very clearly that marriage for life has a huge advantage over a temporary partnership both for men and women ... the only difficulty is that you have to get over the years in between.

CONCLUSIONS

1. Message to women: learn to say no.
2. Message to men: never take no for an answer. Ask a different question.
3. Message to both: keep your eyes wide open before marriage, half shut afterwards. (Benjamin Franklin, *Poor Richard's Almanack*)

Part Three

LOSERS, WEEPERS

10

The Right Answers?

You've found a few more friends to enliven your life. Better still, you've found the Mr. or Ms. Right you've been hoping for and even tied the happy knot. Now how do you keep them from tiring of your company and perhaps roaming off with somebody else? Nobody really knows the answer. Every couple is unique and so is their relationship. Author Anthony Powell suggests that marriage contains 'the moods of a love affair, the contradictions of friendship, the jealousy of business partners, the fellowship of opposed commanders in total war.' (*A Dance To The Music Of Time*)

Easier divorce means that marriage is no longer a lifetime's union. It is more like a formalised, voluntary convenience between a man and a woman for living together. Often neither has a clue what they're getting into. Stricter laws would make it harder to end one marriage and enter another but such restraint is no longer a remedy for a disintegrating partnership. Other guidelines are needed as well as some incentive, financial perhaps, for couples, particularly when they have children.

MULTIPLE CHOICE

In the US, the growth of 'no fault divorces' in the 70s and 80s (later adopted by Britain) was accompanied by a jump of more than 34% in marriage breakdowns over a decade. In an effort to bring down the national divorce rate of 50%, Lenawee County, an hour's drive from Detroit, made every couple planning a wedding take premarital counselling. When Molly Teets and David Harris arranged to marry, they had to answer 165 multiple choice questions ranging over money matters, hopes for children and their sex lives. Having scored well, they were cleared to marry in an old Lutheran church in southern Michigan.

This new regime took effect on 1 June 1997. Though it has no basis in law, Judge James Sheridan agreed with 60 churchmen and the 12 other officials who can conduct marriages in Lenawee County (pop.50,000) not to do so until they had proof that the couples had been counselled. The state of Louisiana followed this lead by introducing a stricter form of matrimony called covenant marriage or 'Marriage Plus' in which the couple promise not to divorce, unless one is found guilty of a biblical transgression such as adultery, desertion or abuse. Marriage Plus is not compulsory but the alternative, the no fault divorce, dubbed 'Marriage Lite', is unlikely to be preferred as it is akin to confessing that the pair are not wholly committed and will split up if things go wrong.

Meanwhile, civil rights groups argue against tougher divorce laws on the grounds that it harms children and the wives of abusive husbands by prolonging bad marriages. The opposite stance is taken by those who say that 'no fault divorces' allow men to walk away from their responsibilities. But the Louisiana experiment is supported by a growing number of other Americans, too. Having grown up in a divorce culture they now think that marriages might be saved through community policies where religious and other leaders try to promote better relationships between couples by encouraging them to get to know each other before marriage. (Not too intimately, one hopes.)

TESTING TIME

In the UK, more efforts are also being made to cement the marriage bond by classes on how to communicate, to avoid conflict and adapt to children. Organised by the counselling charity Relate (www.relate.org.uk) in centres throughout the UK, the classes are targeted at couples planning either to get married, to cohabit or to go into a second relationship – a mix which hardly seems likely to inspire those hoping to walk to the altar with a first time Walter. Advice is also given on such 'touchy' issues (not quite what you think) as who will clean, shop and cook. There are also, sadly but perhaps a necessary concomitant to divorce, advice centres to help children get over the trauma that can result from a parental split.

Some church leaders, including the pastoral care adviser to the Bishop of Oxford, have proposed a church blessing to allow couples to live together before marriage 'to test their vocation'. One is led to wonder what is the care adviser's vocation. The Church of England has condemned this idea of a trial marriage; so did the head of the clergy section of the Manufacturing, Science and Finance Union, saying that betrothals and trial marriages were part of a bygone era. The section's chairman confirmed these sentiments, saying that a trial marriage meant that the woman is more likely to be worse off.

Will any of these attempts prove a deterrent to the mounting tide of divorce, or halt the growing preference for cohabitation rather than marriage? You can't rely on money, youth, beauty or even sexual attraction to keep a man or woman by your side forever, certainly not in the pristine condition in which they once were. Time takes its toll (if it is allowed to) and even the Grim Reaper might turn up unexpectedly to scythe through all your present hopes and future plans.

UNHAPPY PREDICTIONS

Some marriages and relationships are doomed to a Did Not Finish (DNF) finale right from the beginning. The worst are those that have no beginning other than a sexual jaunt, subsequent pregnancy and another child without an acknowledged father. Daughters of divorced parents are more likely to experience a marriage breakup of their own than are sons, or children from an intact marriage. Other factors which predict a DNF ending (but don't always cause it) are:

- **Age**: a woman who marries before the age of 20 is three times as likely to experience divorce as a woman over 20.
- **Money**: poverty increases the risk of divorce; so does the non-pooling of resources; financially independent women are more likely to leave than those who have little money.
- **Work**: arguing about their jobs is a bad sign; so is ambition and spending a great deal of time apart.
- **Sex**: arguing about this presents more of a problem than its frequency. Couples who think that affairs are inevitable and men who put a high priority on physical desirability in a wife are more likely to move off.

- **Depression** can lead to breakups unless there is a great deal of compassion.
- **Expectations** of mutual happiness that are too high are also likely to lead to breakups.

Marriage involves a whole new lifestyle: at a basic level, a routine of sleeping and eating together. It entails far more: considering and caring for another person, forming new loyalties without giving offence to the old – difficult enough with a first, particularly difficult for a second marriage. Since safe contraception became available and pregnancies avoidable, living together seems an easier choice. Take care. It is a far less secure structure than marriage, and breaks down sooner and oftener, leaving more stress in its wake.

Many marriages fail because they are made too hastily, or when a couple are too passionately embroiled to consider the longer term consequences of their actions. It is only later that initial differences such as age, culture or conflicting career patterns turn out to be not so negligible as was at first thought. Against all the early hopes of the couple, the marriage or other relationship drifts towards the rocks. Only if the captain or crew can communicate on the bridge, or even in the cabin, will they save the ship. Teenage marriages are at an increased risk of failure, so are those of couples whose parents have been divorced. When older partners don't stay the course it is usually because if things get difficult, as they always will, it's easier to get out than stay put.

PRESENT IMPERFECT

A good rule to sustain any amicable relationship in work or love is to remember that nobody is perfect and many, possibly even including you, very imperfect indeed. Lower your sights occasionally: don't expect to find an earthbound uncanonised saint to live with you. Some men make wonderful fathers, some wonderful lovers, some wonderful providers, giving freely of their money, time and affection. A woman who wants all these qualities in a husband or lover is living in never-never land. He will have disappeared from the marriage market long ago and be shacked up with somebody who neither deserves nor appreciates him. Don't yearn for or dream about him. He's long since gone and maybe changed for the worse. Be content with your own 'catch'. He may not be everybody's cup of tea. All the better. There's nobody to share him with and you can enjoy his company to the full.

Men, too, dream of a woman who combines the beauty of a film star, the eroticism of a courtesan and the fidelity of a loyal wife. But any woman who is doing a full-time job, organising a household, expecting a baby, dealing with a fractious one, or ferrying children to and from school, is not always going to look like Joan Collins, with never a hair out of place. And would you really expect her to? Robert Herrick declared in his poem *Delight in Disorder* that 'a wild civility do more bewitch me than when art is too precise in every part'. And after all, the more perfect a wife is, the more a husband is likely to seem (though he rarely is) a shadow in her presence.

APPRECIATE THE POSITIVE

So the first rule of a successful relationship is to appreciate the qualities which your man or woman possesses, which drew you to them in the first place and which need mentioning between you now and then to keep them from disappearing. Even when marriages take place for reasons other than mutual affection they can still develop into something worthwhile. When a man or woman is not good at one thing, they are probably good at others.

Focus on the gain, not the loss. Some scientists such as Dr. Dale Griffin of Sussex University believe that people who idealise their partners, seeing them through rose tinted spectacles, stay together longer. Try it. You've nothing to lose. A very good exercise when things seem to be going wrong or at least not quite as smoothly as they might be, is to choose a quiet time, not in the middle of a blazing row, to tell your spouse the things you most like about him or her. Then ask them what they most like about you. Don't be too surprised or disappointed at the answer. You may learn some things you didn't know about yourself.

Compliments never come amiss, either. One of the nicest I ever heard was about a couple, both over 80 and married for some 65 years. Walking over London Bridge they were overtaken by three young skateboarders sailing along and performing the most daring acrobatics. 'Ah,' sighed the man as they passed him, 'sweet bird of youth.' There was a silence between the couple for a few moments, then he looked at his wife and said, 'I might not have the youth, but I've sure got the sweet bird.' Can you think of any compliment nicer than that?

The second force (other than rose tinted spectacles) which binds men and women together in a voluntary lasting union is sharing the same principles or interests and having similar aspirations for themselves and their children. But there is no universal or invincible formula for a happy marriage, except perhaps to keep at it. And if that were easy, the number of divorces could plunge dramatically. Some factors which add cement to a union are:

- a sense of humour
- willingness to compromise
- realising nobody (including yourself) is perfect
- similar religious beliefs.

Another possible way to increase the chance of success is to look at other people's recipes for happy mating. There are two difficulties with this suggestion: (i) the happy couples may divorce before you get a chance to taste their menu; (ii) those who have 'survived' 30–50 years together lived in an era when divorce, if not unthinkable, was certainly more difficult and less commonplace than it is for their children today. However, on the opposite page are recipes given by three different age groups, 30, 40, 50 years, on the do and don't rules they themselves use for a happy partnership.

You might think about having your marriage certificate framed (many children say they have never seen one), and displayed on the wall in the manner of American lawyers or doctors parading their qualifications. The danger here is that the framed certificate might be used as an unholy weapon if tempers ever get frayed. I knew one mother who, at desperation point after months of disturbed nights, threw the baby's feeding bottle at her husband. (The baby is now married herself and her parents are still together.) Had a framed certificate been available, that would doubtless have followed the feeding bottle with more drastic consequences.

Sometimes love at first sight leads to a lasting romance. Well known examples include author Catherine Cookson and her husband Tom. He was a guest in her mother's boarding house in Hastings, and when they met, they knew immediately they were 'made for each other'. More often, rushing into a speedy partnership means you never get time to see each other clearly, to notice any faults, or decide whether you can tolerate them. Everything is clouded with the heady mist of passion.

Recipes for a Happy Partnership

Jane and John 30s,	DON'Ts for John	DO's for John	DON'Ts for Jane	DO's for Jane
known each other six years; lived together two, now married (romantically) for one year; and have a 'passionate' relationship; no children; parents long time married.	promise to do something later and later never comes; promise to be home at a certain time, then come an hour later saying you get caught up with some pals in the pub; leave dirty washing on the floor.	buy me flowers or other occasional gifts; tell me I look good when I'm not sure that I do; drink a glass of wine with me when I'm cooking; offer to do the meal.	nag about leaving dirty washing on the floor; ring me up on my mobile asking when I'm going to be home.	tell me daily that you love me; wear sexy underwear; have fun together; treat me to a candlelit meal occasionally.
Nick and Kate 40s,	DON'Ts for Nick	DO's for Nick	DON'Ts for Kate	DO's for Kate
married 25 years, known each other since childhood; both self employed; children, 14, 11, 5; parents long time married.	plan holidays that aren't relaxing; discuss business late at night; make financial decisions on your own; think you know everything and can't make mistakes.	be my best friend; take me out to dinner at least once a week; assume my priorities are as important as yours; try to get everybody to share the domestic chores; take joint responsibility for the children.	keep worrying; get upset by family untidiness; become moody or complain when business becomes the main priority; ignore my ideas; make financial decisions without mutual agreement.	accept criticism without starting a row; try to be more cheerful when things go wrong.
Jack and Jill 60s,	DON'Ts for Jack	DO's for Jack	DON'Ts for Jill	DO's for Jill
married 30 years, going along nicely until one very low point when Jill's parents split up and depression followed; two children both married.	be a continual prophet of doom; do five minutes' work and spend ten admiring it; choose a TV programme and fall asleep half way through it; drag me round for hours in a DIY store looking for untraceable nails, screws, etc.	listen when I tell you things; be prepared to do things at the spur of the moment; buy surprise presents; take more interest in the social functions I enjoy.	pick up things in shops when it says do not touch; pressure me to do jobs round the house and never praise even a bit, when they're done; get annoyed when (a) I buy a surprise present you don't like (b) you give me a choice of food and then cook something different.	please sometimes buy the first dress you try on rather than try on 20 others and then go back to the first one; do listen to my explanations before erupting or emoting and please switch on brain before opening mouth.

For every couple who married shortly after meeting each other, and are still staying the course after 10 years together, others can be quoted who found love at first sight a recipe for disaster and split up within a year or two.

TROUBLEMAKERS

Three things, however, can be almost guaranteed to lead to trouble. They are (a) alcoholism or other addiction such as drugs or gambling, (b) violence, and (c) adultery. Men and women act in different ways when they are drunk; some become maudlin, some depressed, some violent. All of these can have terrible effects on wives/husbands and any children. So if there are any signs of or gossip about this problem during your dating sessions, think very carefully about starting any liaison whatever. Presuming, however, that alcoholism and its related symptoms show their ugly presence after marriage, what can you do about it?

Alcoholism and other addictions

Get in touch with one of the many services that exist to help those who have an addiction problem. If you love a man or woman enough, you will be able to stand by them. Such loyalty is eminently worthwhile if the partner can pull through. Derek Jameson's wife struggled with her drink problem for 10 years before she sought help but when she did it was the happiest day of their life. 'You need infinite patience,' says this brilliant broadcaster, 'and an absolute refusal to be beaten to see you through.'

Violence

If there are children, put their welfare before any other considerations. Never let them remain in jeopardy from a violent parent. Move. Get help. Try the BBC site (www.bbc.co.uk/health/hh/index.shtml) or the Women's Aid group (www.womensaid.org.uk) who have a list of domestic refuges. Freephone line 0808 2000 247 open 24 hours a day, PO Box 391, Bristol BS99 7WS.

Violence unfortunately sometimes results from mental illness such as schizophrenia, though less often than might be imagined from the media attention it gets. An illness like this which shows itself in a disintegrating personality, thought disturbances and changed patterns of behaviour is, for the sufferers themselves and all who are near to them, a very hard cross to bear. It requires treatment, not always a simple task to arrange. Don't imagine things will get better with peace and quiet or any other easy solution. It won't and if patients don't get the treatment they need (usually medication, which they often refuse to take because of the unpleasant side effects), they will end up either in a police cell because of their odd or occasionally violent behaviour, or be sectioned in hospital for at least six weeks.

Famous psychologist and author Dr. Dorothy Rowe has said that working in psychiatric hospitals, she was horrified to discover that many men scampered off once it became clear that a wife was suffering from severe mental depression or some injury to the brain that meant she could no longer 'fullfil the duties of a wife'. There were also those men 'who would deliver their depressed wife to my office to leave her there with instructions to make her into "the woman I married" '. And there were the quiet heroes who said that they felt part of the problem and wanted to be part of the solution.

Sufferers from mental illnesses need care and support. If you as a spouse can't give it to them (and there may be all sorts of reasons why you may not be able to), make sure at least that they get the attention required. Join an association that helps them. Don't give up on them. Check on their welfare. Depression, too, takes a heavy toll on men and women, though women seem to be more prone to it after childbirth. Patience, love and understanding help the sufferer but sometimes medical or psychological treatment or complementary medicine is also needed.

Illness or death

The death of a child is always a terrible event. Few parents can ever get over it. The grief either tears them apart or welds a family into an even stronger unit. Death underlines the fragility of life and makes everything else, especially impending quarrels, seem unimportant. For some couples, however, especially those whose marriages are already floundering, the death of a child is the final countdown. They just cannot cope with this loss and the devastating effect it has on each other. The marriage collapses.

Illness of the partners, particularly when it is likely to bring long-term care problems into focus, has similar consequences. Some people are able to cope, others not at all. There are numerous charities set up to help with specific conditions, all of which are staffed by a wonderful cadre of specialised workers and volunteers. Use their services. That is what they

are for. Counselling may help, but there is no guarantee that couples can ever adjust to these tragic occurrences in their lives. Every person has to find his or her own solution and salvation.

Adultery

Unfaithfulness (sex with anybody else) or adultery (sex with another's wife or husband) is a hazard that frequently destroys a marriage. Some couples, however, can come to terms with a straying partner and remain apparently devoted to their husbands or less often their wives in spite of their adultery. Examples are many. They range from crowned heads, presidents and other political notables to the more lowly with equally high levels of vanity. If you can cope with this, so be it, but if you can't stand the heat, get out of the bedroom. Arguments about the intrusive effects of jobs can also cause partners to look for sympathy and a bit more elsewhere. Another trigger to adultery can be a job which requires husband or wife or both to spend a good deal of time apart.

Researchers tell us that highly educated men are more likely to have affairs than men with low qualifications. These findings seem fairly obvious: the higher a man's qualifications, usually the better the pay, the greater the power. Such advantages make a big appeal to women. The more attractive you or your spouse are, the more high profile your jobs, and the more public your face, the more likely is temptation to come your way. You will receive adulation, praise, respect (deserved or not) and are more likely to be fêted and made much of, all of which will cause you to be more vulnerable to another person's flattery and charms.

Your friends may turn out to be enemies: near and attractive enough to be invited into your home, your celebrations, to be the right age, have the same kind of outlook, to receive confidences, to flirt at first 'innocently' enough, then to welcome the amatory arm and not so gradually a bit more. Friends like this can be a recipe for disaster. Before your marriage crumbles, call your chef.

Sexual incompatibility

'Senior citizens' are likely to argue that there is no such thing as sexual incompatibility because life is unpredictable and compatibility could quite easily change because of a sudden serious illness or accident in a marriage. They often further argue that being virgins when they got married, as most of them were, added an extra dimension to their partnership: the fun of discovering what bits went where.

Danger points

There is always a point at which no is preferable to a yes, however attractive the yes may be. Don't repeat St. Augustine's prayer, 'Make me chaste, O lord, but not yet'. You're not chaste; you have a wife or husband to whom you've promised to be faithful till death. At certain times in your life this becomes more difficult. When a baby is well on the way, women do not necessarily look their best and after it arrives, they are often too tired to be interested in much else but the demands of the new arrival. A man can feel trapped and unloved and may seek comfort elsewhere just when a woman needs him most.

Life changes

After children leave home or when retirement approaches are other crisis points. Both partners have more free time and fewer domestic responsibilities and may suddenly panic, wondering what they both have in common and how they will fill their days now that they no longer have to consider the children, only each other. Major changes such as this can threaten any marriage. So can redundancy or similar money troubles. If the worries at home are getting too much for you and you are beginning to look elsewhere for solace, ask yourself why. Perhaps you are not getting enough romance/sex from your marriage, or you feel you are being taken too much for granted, not appreciated, your partner is more interested in the job/new car/baby/furniture/DIY/TV, anything rather than you and what you feel or need.

At times like these when the spirit is low, you are more tempted into an affair. Ask yourself what you hope to get from one and how much you will lose. The losses are invariably greater than any gain. Perhaps you are sending out 'available' signals? Playing with fire can be dangerous. Talk your feelings through as far as you can with your spouse. Try to avoid causing hurt or anger.

AVOIDING ARGUMENTS

According to an eminent divorce lawyer, a frequent cause of disputes between couples is that rows keep on even after agreement appears to have been reached. One of the partners continues the argument, perhaps referring to a previous altercation on the same subject. Tempers get overheated, and a slanging match ensues. To avoid this scenario and calm a situation that looks explosive, don't:

- rake up past disputes
- interrupt
- throw out insults
- attack your spouse's character
- make cruel jibes that take a long time to forget and may take many acts of kindness to heal.

Try also not to extend a dispute. If you're complaining for example about a trivial thing like empty toothpaste containers littering the bathroom, keep to the point otherwise this triviality may end up with you (or him) walking out. Be ready to apologise. It is very difficult to put a point of view about which you feel deeply in a brief and sensible fashion. On matters of principle, for example, it must be tried. Timing is important here. Broach the subject after a glass (or a few glasses) of wine or at the end of a well cooked meal. Discuss the pros and cons of your viewpoint, ask for what you want and if it is a good wine or you have learnt the art of skilled negotiating, you're likely to succeed and maybe win a bonus, too.

Professor Howard Markman of Denver University and author of *Fighting for your Marriage* has spent 20 years researching how couples argue. From his observations he declares he can predict who will have a happy marriage and who will not. Marriages likely to end in divorce are those where couples argue by hurling insults at each other and the men tend to withdraw. He suggests that couples have weekly meetings at which they can air their grievances. Such a solution might seem a bit formal for English tastes. In any case, you need not get too downhearted if you appear to be constantly arguing, as long as you heed the warnings above and don't take umbrage afterwards. It may be that you both enjoy this form of communication. Some couples do. They thrive on rows.

Example 1: 'Happy' arguing

When travel writer Eric Newby was in a German prisoner of war camp during World War II, Wanda, an Italian blonde, smuggled him food and messages and helped him escape. Two years later he returned to her and proposed. Fifty years on, they are still married and though devoted to one another, argue incessantly. Wanda reports they have rowed every day they have been together. They never spend time on reconciliations but go on from one argument to the next, yet during Eric Newby's 30 years as a writer, they have not left each other's side.

Example 2: 'Happy' arguing

Britain's longest married couple, Ivy and Fred Farley of Brighton, married aged 18 and 17 years respectively on May 11, 1918. Ivy died in 1996, her husband a few weeks later. Their 78-year marriage survived many arguments, their daughter Joan Webb relates, but adds that a marriage without disagreements is a dull one.

Most arguments, however, usually cause ill feeling and worse. The danger signs are when couples walk away from them entirely or let little disputes grow into big ones. A man is often more physically angered by arguing than a woman is. But if he has learnt a little patience and reacts with a sigh, this helps him to calm down. Looking up as if appealing to God and asking for His divine intervention is no good at all. It is far more likely to bring down earthly wrath upon his head and make the argument even more hurtful. Retreat is no better either. 'I give up' or 'OK. Have your own way … as usual,' is no way to sign off. The wife will feel frustrated that her complaint hasn't been given the time or understanding it merits. Her reaction will be to pursue the matter further and louder.

Other causes of disputes are money, household responsibilities (including child rearing), sex and relatives, especially in-laws. Most of these issues can be discussed before marriage and should certainly be worked out shortly after setting up home together. Unless you feel really strongly on some point, be prepared to lose an argument occasionally.

MONEY TROUBLES

Lack of money is a joint problem, particularly if one partner has it and the other doesn't. Before you come to financial grief (emotional will follow), tackle the problem together. If one is a big spender, open a separate account with standing orders for his or her obligations. Financial arrangements such as a joint account, mortgage arrangements and who pays the bills must be put on a sensible footing, otherwise differences arise which are bound to lead to trouble.

A marriage overrides any previous wills that may have been written. Pensions, too, need some discussion. The law has changed considerably and divorced women are getting a better share of family assets, present and future (too much, some men would argue) but this is no more than just when a wife has looked after children and provided a base from which the husband could achieve a successful career.

Many marriages end in divorce because finances have got out of hand and the couple find themselves heavily in debt. Draw up a budget, itemising your income and expenditure. List all your existing financial arrangements and any debts. From this point, you can decide your financial priorities and how to go forward.

Think twice before putting all your money into a joint current or savings account. With joint accounts, partners are equally liable for debts and overdrafts. This could cause difficulties if you are married to a big spender. The first named in the account will invariably be the husband, and if there are any windfalls or bonuses payable, he will receive them, even if he has left the other named partner long ago and is no longer contributing to the account. However, joint accounts do make day-to-day bill paying easier. Consider opening one specifically for paying bills.

The death of a partner is eased if the rest of the family do not suffer financial hardship. Get adequate cover and make a will. You may also want to consider drawing up a pre-nuptial agreement, detailing who gets what in the event of a split. It's not very romantic but creating such an agreement prior to getting hitched encourages couples to discuss financial matters openly. However comfortable you are about sharing all your worldly goods with your partner now, will you feel the same a few years down the line? When these hazards have been resolved, the smaller but often harder problems can be tackled and so allow you to get the best out of a long and (mainly!) happy life together.

Pearls ... Not Before Time

PROBLEM SOLVING

Men like to solve problems, women to discuss them. So if a woman tells a man of something that is troubling her, the man will try to solve it. She doesn't necessarily want that solution. She just wants somebody to listen to her. He for his part can't understand why if there is a problem it shouldn't be sorted out, and may even give advice on how to do so. Alternatively he may think it's too small, too trifling to discuss, and if his wife grabs him as soon as he comes in to tell him of the piffling problem that concerns her (and adds a few examples of her terrible day), he will soon accuse her of 'nagging'. The evening begins in misery and ends in catastrophe. By listening to a wife's problem, no matter how insignificant it appears, a man shows that he cares. By choosing the right time, a woman gets the attention she needs.

NEVER FROM VENUS ... OR MARS

In his book *Men are from Mars, Women are from Venus*, John Gray gives some excellent advice for 'improving communication and getting what you want in your relationships'. However, looking with English eyes through his somewhat formidable list of '101 Ways to Score Points with a Woman' (offer to build a fire in wintertime; leave the bathroom seat down; offer to make the tea, open the door for her, carry the groceries, heavy loads; change light bulbs when they go out), one wonders what kind of species the American woman is. Judging by this list, she certainly can't come from Venus. If a man from the north of England tried to woo a woman by using some of the tips listed, the response he'd be most likely to get is 'Are you feeling all right, Jack?'

A listening ear

The advice on listening (number 80) sounds somewhat strange: 'reassure her that you are interested by making little noises like ah ha, uh-huh, oh, mmhuh and hmmmm'. My husband added his own 'miaow' to this one. As for number 19: 'when she talks to you, put down the magazine or turn off the TV and give her your full attention', the mind boggles. The American male presumably never listens to a sports channel, such as one relaying football and particularly the World Cup. Can you honestly imagine an English fellow of any age, keen on football, switching off the TV and tuning into some chat in which he hasn't the slightest interest whatever, especially when a goal looks imminent? He might turn off the TV once, or if newly married even twice, but football/rugby lasts two seasons and cricket/tennis follow and sometimes even run in parallel.

One clever advert sums it up. It shows a woman sitting with her back to the TV set at which a friend stares at the match on the screen. Seeing his glued eyes apparently focused on her (does she need bi-focals?) she tells him, 'What I like about you, is that you're such a good listener.' That advert says it all. If you can't make it, fake it and after reading John Gray's 101 ways to woo a woman a man is more likely to rue her than to woo her.

Still, a husband and wife can have great fun doing some chore or other (like shopping, putting in a light bulb) and saying any number that comes into their head, while the other can counter by giving a different number and chore ('making the bed, cooking the dinner'). The number doesn't really matter, it's the laugh that counts.

But Gray is right, listening to your partner is very important. You can often see that somebody is not listening to what you are saying because though they may be looking at you, they seem to be thinking of other things. Good listeners are rare. Become one of them.

Domestic responsibilities

The offer (number 63) to sharpen his wife's knives in the kitchen (the scene of most marital rows!) is hardly likely to inspire a woman with confidence, particularly if the couple are already at daggers drawn. There is some deference to the male ego however in that (number 20) 'if she usually washes the dishes, occasionally offer to wash the dishes, especially if she is tired that day'. Note how certain words like 'occa-sionally', 'tired', 'that day', have slipped in with their implication that the male washing of dishes is not to be thought of as a general rule of masculine behaviour. Surely if this household duty presents a problem as it can when two people are working outside the home, then unless you are in some rural outback, why not buy a dishwasher? It could be more useful and cheaper than a car, which stops you using your feet.

UNDERSTANDING

Men and women have to play so many different roles today, that often they do not know what is expected of them. Neither really understands what the other wants. A woman tends to have more frequent mood changes than a man. She may have seen a TV episode, spoken to a friend, had a row at the office, anything at all can cause a change of mood. If her husband has not been party to the cause he finds this sudden mood swing hard to understand and respond to.

LIES, BIG AND LITTLE

Sometimes a lack of understanding leads to lying or at least to garnish-ing or being economical with the truth. Women's lies tend to be of the softer kind, giving untruthful compliments or praise to save people from hurt. 'Looks lovely on you; thank you for a marvellous dinner; wonderful evening; beautiful colours, etc.' A man lies in this way too, but mainly to bolster up his self confidence. The fact that his wife looks good and is the best at this, that or the other reflects his own taste and good judgement. But if he continually flatters, saying only what he thinks his wife wants to hear, there's going to be Hell to pay when he forgets his role and tells her the truth.

The corollary of this is that if a wife tells her husband she only wants the truth, she must be ready to hear it. The man can soften his approach. Instead of telling her that she looks awful in the dress she thinks is so chic, he can say that he doesn't think she looks so good in this as the red, the blue, etc. – all sorts of ploys to soften the truth, but there is no point in lying. If there can be gradations in lies, the worst type is one to cover up a misdemeanour or bigger fall from grace. The object may be to avoid hurting the partner still more but the subterfuge is going to be hard to explain when the truth surfaces, as it usually does, and makes the truth still more unpalatable.

Dare to be true; nothing can need a lie.
A fault which needs it most, grows two thereby.
(A.P. Herbert)

A man may prevaricate when he is starting or into an affair, or more prosaically when faced with the possible loss of his job or a fall in income. He wants to protect his ego and for the time being at least, avoid 'needless' hurt to his partner. A woman wants to know the situation, otherwise how can she deal with it? And deal with it she will have to. A woman whose job is on the line should also come clean, otherwise who knows, husband and wife might meet each other at the same job interview.

True or false?

A man goes for a very important job interview. If he gets it, the life of his family will radically improve. When he comes home, he tells his wife he has got the job. She gives him a card congratulating him and throws a piece of paper in the waste paper bin. He reads the card and after a rather lengthy embrace, draws back and asks, 'But how did you know I was going to get the job?' 'I didn't,' she tells him and retrieves the crumpled note from the waste paper basket. 'That's what I would have given you if you hadn't got it.' He reads the note in which she consoles him for not having got the job and says she loves him just the same.

Truth is the basis of intimacy in a marriage. Opinions and feelings need to be communicated in as caring a way as possible. They should be the truth, not lies, for whatever reason, but there is no need to treat husband or wife as a Father Confessor, unburdening all your guilt about past (or present) misdemeanours upon their luckless heads. Unless it involves you in some legal/financial commitment (child maintenance for example) or is of direct and current concern to your partner, why should they have to carry your load of guilt? They may react in ways you never imagined and which they and you may long regret. The best solution is if the affair has ended and has no bearing on your present circumstances, say nothing. If the affair is still going on, end it as painlessly as possible, and depending on the temperament of your spouse, keep your mouth tightly shut.

Sheathing the sword of truth in the scabbard of silence

When a husband learnt from his wife, to whom he had been married for 13 years, that she had had an affair with one of his close friends, he was so upset that he reacted very badly over the next few days, once pushing her against a door and twice gripping her by the wrists so tightly that it left a mark. But he was appalled when she left home taking their three children aged nine, seven and five with her to a women's refuge. In spite of the fact that the husband, a deputy headmaster, had no previous history of violent behaviour, his wish for conciliation and promise never to hurt her again, the wife won a ruling that he should leave the house. Two appeal judges refused to overturn that ruling in spite of expressing sympathy for his plight and accepting that it was his estranged wife who 'created' the situation. (Names have been left out from this true story.)

GIVING ADVICE

Associated with the occasional lack of understanding between couples is the giving of advice. Men and women respond differently to advice, a woman taking it more happily than a man does, particularly if it is in a field about which she knows less than he. My husband, for example, is much more experienced in IT than I am, so I welcome any advice I get. His greater knowledge means he would take it amiss if I tried to offer him advice in this field but he is happy to question me about word processing which he uses less often. If one can go from the particular to the general, the moral here is that advice should generally be given only when asked for. This applies to map reading, too – a great bone of contention which can cause havoc on any outing. Get your partner to take a course in orienteering, read the map before leaving home, order better glasses. Never, never say 'I told you so' when a partner makes a mistake that cannot immediately be undone (wrong investment, route, holiday destination or other choice). But if you both feel the same way about an acquaintance, you can enjoy a bit of malicious gossip about them between yourselves ('I always thought he/she wasn't up to much, not to be trusted, a bit odd,' etc.) This won't do much harm, at least to your marriage, and the comparison between them and us will boost both your egos.

SEX

Money problems are sometimes easier to resolve than emotional difficulties. A good sex life is important for a happy marriage, but the fact that demand is unrelated to supply, or vice versa, appears not to be a common cause of marriage breakdown. When they marry, a couple implicitly agree to have sex with each other (although rape within marriage is now a criminal offence). In legal terms, this means a 'reasonable' amount. Excessive demands or a virtual refusal other than by an invalid, will be interpreted as unreasonable behaviour and can justify a petition for divorce. So also will an insistence on contraceptives to avoid having children. Either is likely to drive a partner elsewhere to fulfil their needs. Though a man cannot stop his wife having an abortion if she becomes pregnant, he may be able to use that as evidence of 'unreasonable behaviour' for divorce, but in today's climate, he will need a good advocate to prove it.

Marriage without sex

Steven Rimmer, a 45-year-old computer technician, met Vivien, a 37-year-old lab technician, through their interest in pet rats. (Hardly the most romantic subject, one would think, but it shows how wrong you can be.) A series of meetings ensued, often by chance, followed by an old fashioned courtship. He summoned up the courage to propose but after the wedding at a Catholic church, she said she had never slept with anyone and wanted to get used to the idea. She apparently did not get used to it, but kept to her own bedroom, and the marriage deteriorated. Counselling was of no help, and two years after the marriage, though he still loved her, they were divorced.

MAKING YOUR SPOUSE FEEL SPECIAL

A woman wants to feel cherished, secure in the knowledge that her husband cares for her. She needs continual reinforcement of his love, a hug or two, a compliment about what she is wearing, her birthday (or an anniversary) remembered appropriately and occasional acts of kindness unrelated to anything. A man makes a big gift and thinks that's the end of it until next Valentine's Day, 100 points say, whereas 20 points at five a time would be more appreciated. When a woman does not get this affection, it may cause her to view more tenderly the affections of another man and possibly to leave her husband for him. If the new love is younger than she, this is a wonderfully exhilarating step until the cookie crumbles as in the nature of things it surely will. It is many a young man's dream to tumble into bed with even a half beautiful but experienced older woman. The dream does not last forever, and the woman who makes it come true will have to pay the price when he leaves her for a younger beauty, as he almost inevitably will.

As for older men, married or single with not quite honourable intentions, they will flatter you, tell you how special you are, that you're the one they've been waiting for all their life (or some such tale) and many other niceties that your husband has forgotten to mention in the last weeks or months. You say you won't be tempted; seeing this possible paramour a few times won't do anybody any harm; it's only a bit of fun; you won't go all the way, etc., but almost before you know what's hit you, you're down and out. Lies will not cover up the deception forever; the new love (old hat for him) will go, and you are almost certainly bound for the First Wives Club and its pool of tears.

Not quite the same fate awaits a husband who has an affair with another woman. Though he may also find a new bedmate stimulating, the exhilaration will be mixed with guilt. He risks divorce and all the acrimony that goes with it. When there are children, he also risks losing them for the time being, and possibly for ever. If his wife (partner) is of the forgiving type, he may get a reprieve, but he can't rely on it. Before he goes off on his peregrinations, let him ask himself: is your journey really necessary? Commitment means faithfulness and obviates the need for lies.

WHEN TWO BECOME THREE OR MORE

Husbands as well as wives want to feel loved, admired and desired. This is particularly true after the arrival of the first child. At that time the father sometimes feels that he is being pushed out from his former cosy relationship, that his wife no longer has time for him, she is almost obsessed with the new arrival. Yet she may actually be exhausted with the demands of this newcomer into the family home and all the learning process that a first child brings in its wake.

Share the baby and at least some of its needs between you. Parents are people, with needs of their own, too. Some of these are very demanding, and cannot easily be ignored or given up without in some cases creating mayhem and worse. How often do doctors stay away from their practice to help their wives with a new baby? For how long does a broadcaster/journalist covering an outbreak of violence in a war zone ask for paternity leave? What about men in the armed forces? With some jobs, a woman may have to put up with a man's absence at crucial times in their joint lives like the birth of a child.

Fathers in jobs like this, which involve frequent or unexpected moves, may have to be away not only for the important birth of a child, but from comparatively minor events (though not to the children) like school activities including plays, parents' evenings and sports days. Women who cannot face these absences on the part of their husband should never opt for a man in these jobs. Men, too, have to decide whether, to be nearer their families, they will give up work for which they may have trained over a long period and which they enjoy. In some cases, employers can help by making absences, like paternity leave, easier to arrange, though the high level of sick leave in many firms does not bode well for genuine need.

Whatever you read about so called single parents, there is no such thing (except in the creed of the Catholic church) as a virgin birth. Your child has been created by two people. Both parents have a right (and a duty) to share its upbringing. Encourage the father to bath and dress his child. Don't worry how inept he is. You weren't so good yourself when your child arrived and only the bit of practice you had thereafter has given you the edge on your husband.

Staying the course

If the new arrival cannot tell the time and does not recognise the difference between night and day, and you feel you are getting desperate for want of sleep or are being edged out by this newcomer, don't flee the nest. Unless, in spite of all your efforts to stay together, life has become unbearable, make splitting up your last move not your first. For many children, a parental split can be more devastating and harder to accept than death itself. Children rarely if ever feel guilt when a parent dies, but if their father or mother leaves the family home, they may rack their brains for months wondering if it was their fault that Mummy or Daddy left them. When their parents are married rather than living together, there is a more obvious bond.

So think long and hard before deciding on a separation. You can both change and probably both have but that isn't a reason for going your separate ways. Nobody is going to satisfy all your physical and emotional needs. Your partner probably knows them better than anybody else. Bring them back into focus.

Never mind that all your friends are boasting of their wonderful new lover(s), or that they are into their second or third relationships, or so they say. Never mind what high society is doing; ignore the antics of pop stars. They haven't got your child/ren. It may be far from the perfect solution for you and your spouse to stick together but it is likely to be the best in the long run. The average short run today lasts a mere two years. One in ten couples head for the courts after 24 months. It is not even necessary to go for the court. A big superstore has come out with a cheap 'Divorce Kit' which saves you the cost.

B Ys with your Xs (be wise with your exes – and kindly, too)

Don't assume that divorce is the one remedy for a breakdown in communication or that 'moving on' will improve your lot. If after all your efforts to keep together you really have to split, make an effort when time has mended the wounds a little to keep a relationship going with those who stayed behind when you 'moved on'. That you could not continue to live as husband and wife should not mean that you cannot remain friends, particularly if you run a business together. Fathers and mothers are not the only ones who suffer from losing access to children. In-laws, grandparents and other relations also do.

Try not to resort to the fast growing American custom of a terminator – a person hired to phone and end an unwanted relationship. Deanna Thompson, founder of one such organisation (breakupservice.com) ends about 50 romances a month. Because there are so many more services bringing people together, breakupservice.com has to do a lot more work. 'Emotionally draining' comments Deanna unemotionally. The go-betweens use sweet voices and honeyed words for the execution that the real terminators are too cowardly to perform in person. But as is sometimes the case (not always, one is happy to add), England follows America, so this un-English custom could take root here much more easily than the American Silver Ring Thing: teenage abstinence before marriage.

SOME LAST GUIDELINES

Guidelines for happy families do not begin with 'for richer for poorer' (take richer); 'in sickness and health' (take health) nor 'till death (or divorce or a better catch) do us part'. Commitment is needed, so is talking and listening to each other, respect for the views expressed, loyalty, a sense of humour and above all, the guts and patience to stick it out through the bad times when a malevolent fate takes charge, as at some time, it invariably will.

It helps cohesion for meals to be family affairs round a table, at least a few times in the week if you can't manage more, not stuck in front of the TV screen with a plate of sandwiches on your lap. Exceptions can be made for mutually agreed programmes. Provide firm guidelines for children. Check on the computer use (www.youngpersonsguide.co.uk is a handy book to have around). Even when children don't keep within the parameters set for them (and older ones probably won't), better that they should know what the rules are, than to have none at all. At least they'll know the score.

Finally, when times get really tough, as they sometimes do, it's useful to remember that if you join an organisation like the police, the army, the marines, the navy, you have to learn to get on with those near to you. You live with them, eating and often sleeping alongside them. If you don't get on with your colleagues in this enforced situation, you endure a miserable existence until you can get out. That may seem like a very long time indeed, and you can easily go from the frying pan into the fire. The same can be said of an uncommitted relationship. You get on or you fall out.

Marriage is, or should be, happier and longer lasting. It is about love for each other and for any children that arrive. Think of it as a marathon, not a sprint. Or liken it to an investment in a good but unfledged company that has growth prospects. There may be very few payments in the early years, the price falls and you seem to be waiting for dividends in vain. Give your investment time. A different one may be no better and could prove far worse. So it is with marriage. Stay the course. Find and keep the right man or woman and you will enjoy (as the religious might add, with God's help) a lifelong, fulfilling and truly rewarding relationship.

Index